D0992445

Win at Work!

Win at Work!

The
EVERYBODY WINS
Approach to Confliction Resolution

DIANE KATZ, PhD

WILEY

John Wiley & Sons, Inc.

Published by John Wiley & Sons, Inc., Hoboken, New Jersey.
Published simultaneously in Canada.

For general information on our other products and services or for technical support, please contact our Customer Care Department within the United States at (800) 762-2974, outside the United States at (317) 572-3993 or fax (317) 572-4002.

Wiley also publishes its books in a variety of electronic formats. Some content that appears in print may not be available in electronic books. For more information about Wiley products, visit our web site at www.wiley.com.

Library of Congress Cataloging-in-Publication Data:

Katz, Diane, 1946-
  Win at work! : the everybody wins approach to confliction resolution / Diane Katz.
    p. cm.
  ISBN: 978-0-470-59917-4 (cloth)
  1. Conflict management. 2. Communication in organizations. 3. Interpersonal relations. 4. Interpersonal communication. I. Title.
  HD42.K38 2010
  650.1'3—dc22

                                                                  2010007794

Printed in the United States of America

10 9 8 7 6 5 4 3 2 1

For JLC
The light of my life and the hope of my heart.
Thanks to Mom and Dad, for always believing in me.
Wish you were here.

Contents

Introduction

Understanding Conflict at Work

How often do we find ourselves stuck with or frustrated by conflict at work? Far too often! After years of watching organizations struggle to free themselves from destructive conflict, I developed The Working Circle, a step-by-step process that helps men and women resolve workplace conflict in a nonconfrontational, creative, and collaborative way.

Conflict by itself is neither good nor bad. It just is. We can't avoid it; it emerges in every aspect of our lives, every single day, to a greater or lesser extent. Imagine having no conflict at work. At first, you might think what a wonderful experience that would be! But that would be true for a very short period of time; after a while, it would get boring. Why? Because conflict gets our juices flowing; it motivates us to excel. Competition is conflict, after all, and in the business world, we certainly need to be competitive! Without conflict/competition, there would be fewer opportunities for creative thinking, breakthroughs, innovation, and professional growth.

Conflict: Constructive and Destructive

There are two kinds of conflict at work: destructive and constructive. Destructive conflict distracts you from achieving the goals of the organization; it takes your eyes off the prize and puts more focus on "covering your butt." If you have a disagreement with someone, for example, most likely you will not resolve the conflict. Instead, you are more likely to talk about that person and the problem to other people, in an attempt to gain allies rather than find solutions.

At one Fortune 100 company where I worked, things weren't going very well. Revenues were down, the stock price was plummeting, and morale was at an all-time low. The fear of layoffs was prevalent, causing productivity to drop. Execs were under constant pressure to perform—to survive. Instead of an atmosphere of collaborative teamwork, an "every man for himself" attitude took over. People began exhibiting negative behaviors with regularity; colleagues provided insufficient data to one another; teams were pitted against each other; and lying became widespread. In response, leaders looked the other way, because they were struggling to survive, too.

The preceding is a case study in destructive conflict. Instead of assembling the tools necessary to compete effectively in the marketplace, internal deception and conflict took over, with the majority of employees following personal agendas, which often were inconsistent with organizational goals.

Constructive conflict, in contrast, generates creativity, problem-solving behaviors, improvements, and innovation. In such an environment, not only is it okay to disagree, it's encouraged! Disputants deal directly with each other, typically using a common language or process, such as the one I provide in The Working Circle. Moreover, constructive conflict invites healthy internal competition, whereby everyone collaborates and shares in the rewards of success.

For constructive conflict to exist in the workplace, however, everyone must know what the company's goals are, be willing to work hard to accomplish them, and support the efforts of others. And when there is a battle for resources, it is undertaken openly, so as to rally assistance and provide all the necessary supporting data. In this way, internal competition becomes an opportunity to excel and to cooperate.

We're all aware that conflict can provoke fear, anger, resentment, and hesitation, particularly when the consequences might affect our ability to succeed at work. The Working Circle allays those concerns by offering a reliable approach for addressing these negative responses, one that combines emotional intelligence with common sense, enabling you to move with confidence from conflict to resolution.

The Cyclical Nature of Conflict: No Beginning, No Ending

One of the strengths of The Working Circle approach is its flexibility. As opposed to linear models, it has no beginning and no ending. It is designed as a circle, meaning the eight component steps can be revisited multiple times, until a satisfactory resolution to a conflict has been reached. Think about it: Doesn't it seem clear that there is no end to conflict? Throughout history, there have been peaceful times and there have been times of conflict. Both peace and conflict are cyclical, not linear. One event leads to a consequence, which leads to another event, and so on.

In business, we face complex questions, not only about revenues, but about independence, ethics, marketing, research, strategies, and leadership. To help you learn how to deal with all types of business questions, this book offers real-life examples of professionals at pivotal points in their careers. It reveals how to circumnavigate the roadblocks that can otherwise stop you in your tracks. It will help those of you who are uncomfortable dealing with conflict, giving you a tool that precludes confrontation. For those of you who tend to be aggressive as a normal course of action/response, The Working Circle will help you learn to respond in a much more collaborative and approachable manner. And for those of you who simply don't know what to do in the face of conflict at work, The Working Circle will empower you with the language and process you need to achieve relatively painless resolutions to conflict.

Decision Making: The Traditional Masculine Model

Early in my career, I observed that one of the reasons conflict doesn't get resolved effectively in organizations is due to the traditional male model of decision making. We "attacked" issues; competition was analogized to war; when someone was fired, he or she was said to have been "terminated." In short, conflict at work was all about aggression; about who would come out "on top." Thus, decision making, the cornerstone of conflict resolution, was done in an oppositional manner. Opposing sides gathered their allies, who then situated themselves for strategic advantage. If anyone tried to introduce collaboration as a tactic, the suggestion was often disregarded, or the person raising the possibility was viewed as lacking a grasp of what business is all about.

Let me give you a stereotypical example of the difference between the masculine and feminine approaches to decision making. I had reason to visit an orthopedic center, where many orthopedic surgeons are housed in one building, with a large, communal administrative support staff. In the United States, there are very few female orthopedic surgeons, so it was not surprising to find that most of the surgeons at this center were men.

(Please keep in mind here that I am offering a stereotype, and although some stereotypes have a basis in fact, rarely will everyone in any given group fit the stereotype.)

I was told by my friend using this center that the surgeons there practice the typical male model of surgical service; that is, no-nonsense advice and care, and no soft interpersonal skills. On the other hand, the support staff (primarily female), are helpful, but are given no empowerment. On one occasion, my friend asked one of the women on the support staff a question—which, it turned out, required a low level of authority to answer. She told my friend that she was not allowed to answer and, further, that no doctor was available to provide an answer. Thus, my friend could not get a reply to her fairly simple request.

This is an actual, though extreme, example of how the masculine and feminine sides of organizations can be at odds and create conflict. As a result of this bifurcation at the orthopedic center, the service patients receive there is often less than stellar. The two sides do not communicate effectively, and that is a prescription for mistakes.

In this case, the two sides don't communicate effectively because they have limited expectations of one another. The doctors (the masculine side) expect to be "right"; the support staff (the feminine side) expect to be "wrong." The women expect to give help to the doctors; the doctors expect to get help from the support staff. If, instead, they talked to each other, really communicated, resulting in a more balanced distribution of power, both groups would have more and better information, enabling everyone at the center to make speedier and more accurate, effective decisions; provide greater service; and avoid costly mistakes. And the patients would feel welcomed and reassured that they were receiving the best care possible.

This example is in no way intended as an indictment of either the masculine or the feminine approaches to decision making, just as a very clear illustration that all organizations need both. I am referring here, of course, to the qualities, not the genders. I have worked with balanced organizations that had a majority of either men or women; they achieved balance because they incorporated both aspects of leadership to make decisions and resolve conflicts.

Who's the Victor?

Too often today, organizational conflict is viewed as who will be the victor, who will win, as opposed to looking at the merit contained in both sides of the issue. Consequently, conflict is nonproductive, taking employees' minds off accomplishing the goals of the organization and, instead, setting those minds to work devising strategies for survival.

We had a joke at one company I worked for: "Keep your back away from the door. You never know who's going to come in and stab you!" I spent so much time figuring out ways to watch my back that it was debilitating. I have no doubt you understand what I'm talking about, how much energy it can take, to a greater or lesser degree, to dodge bullets being fired at work.

When an organization is skilled at conflict resolution, it can take place with learning, creativity, and a cooperative letting-go. But too often what happens is that one side or person is the victor, and the vanquished either moves into the shadows, shamefully disempowered, or leaves the company. In the latter case, it could mean the loss of valuable resources and knowledge. When there is only the *appearance* of resolution, initially there is a collective sigh of relief, and the desire to "just move on" prevails; rarely does anyone ask how to avoid similar conflict in the future. This is an overwhelming male model, and as history continues to repeat itself, highly unproductive.

One aspect of recent events ("I want more for me no matter what the overall results are") is an example of dominance in conflict, *not* collaboration. For numerous reasons, organizations have lost the "we" approach to doing business. What is left is "I": I want, I need, and so on. I used to interview MBA graduates, and was struck by how many of them would ask what they would get, and forget to ever mention what they could contribute.

Taking the journey described in this book allows both men and women to experience a model for conflict resolution that is balanced between the essential masculine qualities of planning, focus, and assertiveness with the equally important feminine attributes of collaboration, creativity, and willingness to support.

The Working Circle has been called "one of the most supportive, creative, and flexible systems available to professionals." As such, it can be used to address any conflict at work, and at every stage of your working life. You will find it as valuable to you in the uncertain early days as a new hire as when you are enjoying the rewards and managing the responsibilities as a CEO. The eight-step process will help you get unstuck when facing a difficult decision, and help you move forward with confidence, enhancing your ability to demonstrate the leadership qualities that count for so much among your peers.

As you become more familiar with this amazing technique, you will join the thousands of my clients who use this program whenever they need to move through an impasse. Each of the questions posed in the book can reveal exactly where your sticking point may be and help release you from it.

Remember, when you choose *not* to resolve a conflict, you are making a decision that has an impact on both the situation and your self-esteem! Fortunately, your first decision was to read this book. How soon will you be faced with a conflict to resolve? Will you be ready? With the help of The Working Circle, you can be assured that any future conflicts you face will be less of a drain on your time and energy, and your self-confidence will grow!

PART ONE

PART ONE

WHAT IS THE WORKING CIRCLE?

Chapter 1

The Power of the Circle in Conflict Resolution

I work with organizations of every kind and size and I never cease to be amazed at how rarely companies offer emotionally intelligent processes for resolving conflicts. Think about it: Have you ever, when you started a new job, attended a seminar that explains "how we resolve conflicts here"? I'd be surprised if your answer were yes. Most of the time employees are told by management, "We are a team here!" For some reason, companies seem to expect their employees to come to the job knowing instinctively which steps to take to address challenges they face on the job. If there is training on this important topic, it tends to be idealized, and fails to make a direct connection to the actual culture of the organization.

Why People Have Problems Resolving Conflicts

In my experience, very few organizations can articulate the most effective (and *realistic*) approach to problem solving and conflict resolution, even though employees are called upon to use this skill every single day. If a manager does say, "Okay folks, we've got to stop the bickering, and get along here," there's rarely even a hint as to how to stop the bickering, beyond the nondescript "behave and get along" type of instruction. If an attempt is made to get to the cause of the conflict, it usually results in assigning blame. Once there is an assignment of blame, opposing sides resort to blame avoidance and reluctance or refusal to take responsibility. I call this the "no-stick" approach to work—the effort to bounce blame off of oneself and attach it to someone else. How often do you read e-mails or sit at meetings in which people use techniques to avoid blame or responsibility for some blowup or failure? Worse yet, how often does someone attempt to lay blame or assign negative responsibility directly on your shoulders?

Everyone expects the other person to learn how to behave, because no one feels safe enough to assume responsibility. We end up feeling victimized at work, and thus have a hard time seeing our own behavior in any sort of objective light. Responsibility comes to mean not courage and ownership, but blame. Under these circumstances, we have a hard time trusting the people we work with. At the end of the workday, we are exhausted, and the exhaustion isn't from our work, but from dodging bullets. This typically happens to a greater or lesser degree, but at whatever level it does occur, we start to expect that this is what work is about. That brings disengagement, and, over time, both the professional loses and the organization loses.

When destructive conflict occurs, the informal network works overtime, with more gossip ensuing, thereby deepening the polarization. In more extreme cases, disputants can undermine each other's efforts. And if the position of leadership is to assume that everyone will get along better in the future, or that this is just what happens at work, it's not surprising that everyone comes to expect that what happened in the past will continue in the present, that this is the status quo.

Consequently, when it comes to resolving long-standing conflicts at work, most people rely on their personal styles for doing so, which they probably developed when they were kids. Coping styles learned in childhood are generally not flexible, and rarely are useful in the workplace! Professionals who have had training in conflict management skills commonly have been taught to focus on a linear, combative model to support their efforts. The training, moreover, usually is idealized, and fails to use as examples real situations about real people, which could help them when they are in the trenches. To date, no organization I have been called in to work with was factoring the company culture into the teaching of conflict resolution skills. For example, some cultures are more aggressive than others; working at them *requires* assertive management skills. In more nonconfrontational cultures, by contrast, employees need to use indirect language. Thus, the training I provide for, say, construction workers, must be different from the training I offer to social workers. The concepts are the same, but the situational language used has to shift.

Conflict and Culture

Conflict and culture are very closely related. Figuring out the culture where you work is, for most people, an intuitive activity, and not so much a conscious one. In my case, however, I enjoy observing human behavior, and have been studying organizational cultures for a very long time, in a very conscious manner. For example, when I began working at Chase, I immediately noted how everyone dressed; it quickly became clear to me that the bank had an unwritten dress code. I would sit at meetings and look at everyone's shoes. Most of the men (this was in the 1980s) wore wingtip shoes, with tassels. And in those days the men all wore suits. When a man was in his office, he would take his suit jacket off, and hang it up. If he had to leave his office (sometimes just to go to the men's room), he would put the jacket on. Within two months of being hired, all male employees had adopted the dress code, and the custom, sometimes without conscious thought. Culture imposes conformity and uniformity to rules—many of them unspoken.

Let me give you another example of corporate culture, from a large engineering firm. All the male employees at this firm wore slacks and shirts with collars. Further, what I noticed as I began to visit on a regular basis, was that they wore just two shirt colors: blue (many shades) and white. When men came to work there, they learned on a subliminal level which colors were acceptable to wear. Therefore, in a short period of time, no colors other than blue and white were being worn.

What Unspoken Rules Exist in Your Workplace? Connecting culture to conflict requires taking a leap, but one that is important to make, if you want to succeed at your company. Here's an example of that connection I witnessed at a large law firm, where it was accepted (and almost expected) that once an attorney made partner, he or she was free to make accusations, shout, and have angry fits. And if the partner was an impressive revenue generator, he or she had even greater license to behave badly. Prior to becoming a partner, it was totally not acceptable to demonstrate such behavior. What message did that send? To aspiring attorneys, the freedom to act poorly was seen as a reward.

Conversely, for the nonattorney staff, there was a persistent belief that being the poorly treated underclass was a condition of employment.

As a result of this kind of culture, conflict resolution becomes unbalanced: it functions entirely under the male model. It always makes me smile to think that attorneys are trained to be adversarial, and that this is also how they generally manage and behave. Of course, I have met some attorneys who are outstanding managers, but law firms normally support cultures that feed on destructive conflict.

Another example indicative of the connection between conflict and culture comes from a large national nonprofit, where conflict is viewed as something to avoid. People there smile a lot, gossip a lot, avoid direct conversation a lot. If there is a conflict that won't go away (which happens frequently), the disputants are treated more in a therapeutic manner. Tiptoeing around the source of the conflict is the norm, as is discussing the conflict with one's allies around the coffee machine. When I have asked disputants about their adversaries, I generally get a response like, "I really like her; I think we can get along. I don't really know what the problem is. Can we talk about something else now?" This is a classic illustration of the feminine model of avoidance, which over time sucks the energy right out of an organization.

No leader in any organization would openly admit that conflict is encouraged, and that collaboration is discouraged. Unwittingly, however, cultures develop that do exactly that, and then the reward systems emerge that maintain the status quo. The point is, leaders need to be equally comfortable sustaining constructive conflict and collaboration.

I have worked with many professionals involved in messy conflicts, who want to resolve them professionally, and effectively—such as protesting an action of a manager, requesting more teamwork, or asking for a more balanced workload. But for most individuals, the simple act of facing management usually leaves them feeling nervous, insecure, and unclear as to what to say and how to best approach the more senior staff member.

As I've said before, most corporations are run in a very male-oriented manner. Demonstrating dominance, denying mistakes, taking no prisoners, being solution focused, and so on, are all common behaviors I see in most businesses. These are not negative qualities; on the contrary, most of them are necessities for success. But there are subtleties involved.

In a competitive world, one needs to demonstrate dominance, yes, but always having to do this implies always having to be on top, always having to prevail. That is impossible. What does a company do when it is not victorious? It needs to rely on feminine qualities, like adapting and admitting to mistakes. Organizations that just keep charging forward inevitably exhaust their employees; they don't use reflection as a learning tool, and thus foster combative cultures. Everything becomes colored by the "I'm right, you're wrong" attitude. (Does that sound like the way our government is run, too?)

Companies that invoke feminine traits such as process orientation, mutual support, admission of mistakes, and submission are in the minority. That said, these behaviors are not necessarily positive, either, all the time or in every circumstance. As I noted in the Introduction, neither set of behaviors in and of itself is negative; it is the imbalance that is negative. It is the degree to which any organization relies on either masculine or feminine behaviors that puts it in balance or out.

One surefire way to determine where your organization is on the masculine/feminine continuum is to examine the jokes that travel around the office. Joking that is aggressive, that revolves around insiders and outsiders that makes some people uncomfortable, usually reflects a more masculine culture. I was at breakfast at a conference held by a large national organization where there was entertainment—or what some people thought was entertainment. The comedian went on for about 10 minutes telling jokes and making comments about how dumb people from Oklahoma were. I did not find him funny at all, but I couldn't help but see that the humor reflected the culture of the organization—elitist, opinionated, and separatist. And, as exemplified by the aggressive manner of the comedian, it was certainly masculine.

Let me sum up this section by sharing with you an interesting and amusing comparison that was making the rounds a while ago about three different companies on Wall Street, specifically about how each of them operated. (For obvious reasons, I won't reveal their names):

Company #1: "Ready, fire, aim!" (The masculine model)

Company #2: "Ready, ready, ready!" (The feminine model)

Company #3: "Ready, aim, ready, fire!" (The balanced model)

Which One Is Your Organization? As I write these thoughts, I am faced with a dilemma: as a woman, how do I present these ideas without appearing to condemn masculine traits? In order to be as successful as I have, I have had to develop many masculine qualities. On the other hand, I never was, or even wanted to be, so masculine in my behavior that I forgot to be feminine, to exhibit compassion and be willing to admit my mistakes, even to my adversaries.

This is the balance I've been talking about, which organizations need. It doesn't matter what the establishment is about, whether it is a corporation, the government, a nonprofit, or a small entrepreneurial venture. It could be your supermarket, your city government, your church, or the nonprofit you donate to. When there is balance between masculine and feminine attributes in an organization, that organization will compete, thrive, display compassion, be creative, be nimble, be able to resolve conflicts with accountability, and thus be a great place to work.

The Working Circle is a balanced approach, opening up both masculine *and* feminine perspectives, so that solutions to problems and conflicts are far more comprehensive and longer lasting.

As I've said before, usually we think of conflict resolution as a linear process—there's a beginning and an ending—and organizations and individuals tend to favor this viewpoint, as limited as it is. Because it is limited, there are definite disadvantages to using it. For one, a linear approach erroneously assumes you'll find a solution by following a straight line of thinking. However, when you confine yourself within the limits of linear thinking, you're less likely to think outside the box (solve problems creatively).

When creativity is encouraged, people tend to be more courageous in generating ideas; they are more collaborative, too, even in the midst of conflict. Recall from the Introduction that I said decision making is the foundation of resolving any conflict. The decision-making process, at its best, is creative and nonlinear. In fact, there is no beginning or ending to decision making, for once we make a decision there are consequences. Those consequences then lead to the need to make more decisions, and on and so on. You get the idea.

In contrast to the beginning-and-ending process, a nonlinear approach allows us to meander around ideas, explore more options, and become more creative with our solutions. A nonlinear approach also lets us explore using our intuition, taking into account our emotions, hunches, and gut feels; these represent the feminine side of the decision-making process. We are all familiar with using the masculine, straight-to-the-finish way of making decisions. I'm suggesting that by combining the linear with the more intuitive (circular) approach, we can all become extraordinary decision makers. This is true whether you are a man or a woman. When making decisions, we need all the tools (feminine and masculine) available to us—especially at work, where competitive pressures abound.

As we progress as professionals and face the many cross-roads that appear throughout our careers, we need a conflict resolution process that will serve us at every fork in the road. And that's the beauty of The Working Circle—it delivers!

One of the primary reasons The Working Circle is so effective is that it factors in intuition as a vital component in decision making. Despite proclamations made by some business gurus that intuition is alive and functioning well in organizations, in practice most companies fail to support its use in the conference and boardrooms, preferring the tried, but not so true, linear approach.

Understandably, the masculine, linear decision-making model fits comfortably within the traditional male-dominated business structure. The gender imbalance naturally fostered an out-of-balance decision-making process. But one of the consequences of that continuing imbalance is the loss of maximum creativity, which can put companies at a serious disadvantage; simply put, creative organizations are known to develop competitive advantages. Sad to say, however, in the last 20 years, even as women have been steadily rising in the corporate ranks, the balance has not yet shifted dramatically: the masculine decision-making model still prevails. Why? Because women have felt the need to assume masculine attributes and characteristics in order to succeed and fit in with established company cultures.

The Working Circle proposes that following a circle (a more feminine shape), rather than a line, will enable you to include the intuitive with the linear, the masculine and the feminine. Keep in mind, in business, balanced decision making, which leads to effective and creative conflict resolution, is a necessity, not a luxury.

When we use a process that engages both our masculine and feminine sides, we can excel in new ways. This is what The

Working Circle offers: new ways to excel. Women using this process tap into their intuition more openly, thus offering richer, more well-rounded perspectives and information when considering complex issues. Men using this process can expand on and extend their linear, masculine take on issues by adding the ability—and willingness—to be collaborative and creative.

We all have both feminine and masculine aspects to our personalities, and by learning to incorporate them in our dealings with one another, we can expand our ability to reach out to each other in new and more effective ways.

Where Does Destructive Conflict Come From?

Let's face it, conflict and work go together, and conflict of a destructive nature (as opposed to the constructive form) takes our focus away from doing the job we are paid for and shifts us into political maneuvering. Whenever I conduct an organization assessment (the process of figuring out what makes an organization succeed or stumble), I ask the question, "What's the culture like here?" More often than not, the response is something vague like, "It's crazy here!" Everyone absorbs the culture, but few can really articulate its norms and unwritten rules. This is unfortunate, because it is these norms and unwritten rules that describe the values of the organization much more accurately than any plaque on the wall or on your desk given to you by the company.

Just where does all that craziness come from? From observing organizations ranging from government agencies to academic institutions to churches to corporations, I have come up with a list of the primary sources of all that debilitating conflict:

1. *Poorly designed jobs*. Jobs that have overlapping responsibilities and ill-defined accountabilities leave workers

scurrying to achieve and compete needlessly. In other words, you and your coworkers think that what has to be done resides with each of you. Or, worse, none of you think it is your job. Either way, the people involved begin to view each other with mistrust and resentment. Management either takes sides or sees the employees themselves as the problems to be solved, rather than the job descriptions. Few in the organization see the root cause is actually job design, so the individuals involved remain in a conflict that can't be resolved.

2. *Unrealistic orientations.* If your company's orientation is about filling out forms and adding up the number of hours you worked, and telling you how many hours you are scheduled to work, along with policies and more policies, it is insufficient and ineffective. Orientations that don't give you what you *really* need to know about what it takes to succeed ("Working long hours goes a long way here"), and what the culture is *really* like ("We want you to settle your own conflicts") don't help people to succeed and learn. I've seen executives come to orientations and talk about what a great place the company is, and how risk-taking is encouraged. They forget to mention what happens to people who fail or disagree with the party line. Ouch!

3. *Win-lose compensation plans.* Usually compensation plans are designed to increase profit and reward performers. So far so good. But sometimes the plan pits divisions and/or people against each other. As much as some executives enjoy and promote this approach, it encourages destructive conflict. Data flows if the lifeblood of organizational success, but, under this model, people don't share necessary information with each other. The

quintessential example is the shoe store where the sales-people are all on commission. When you walk in, they attack you as if you were a deer in the forest and they were the hunters. Ugh!

4. *Managers who mean well but don't know how to manage conflict.* You've met them; we all have. They gossip with you about your coworkers, and in doing so feed the fires of conflict. A manager should *never* participate in office gossip, as taking sides empowers one position and weakens the other. Managers may be conflict avoiders themselves, doing whatever it takes to steer clear of any confrontation, in an effort to maintain the peace and/or to be liked. Or they simply don't know how to handle difficult employees and by not dealing with them let them, in essence, run the shop. This type of manager is extremely frustrating, because, of course, the general employee population expects them to lead, not allow the bullies or whiners to take charge. Most of the time, these well-meaning but unskilled managers are likeable, yet hapless. The good news is, they are usually not hopeless—if the organization recognizes the problem and provides intensive coaching for the managers who need it.

5. *Training programs that aren't reinforced.* In companies across the United States, billions of dollars are spent on training programs each year. As far as I'm concerned, most of it is wasted. Why? When was the last time you went to a training class and, afterward, your manager asked you what the class was about and what he or she could do to reinforce what you had learned? Other than technical training, the skills that are taught at such programs are rarely reinforced in practice. Here's an example: I was teaching front-line supervisors basic

supervisory skills, and a week after the class concluded, was talking to one of the participants. He told me he really enjoyed the class, after which I asked him how his manager felt about what he had learned. Here's what he said his manager told him: "Forget what they taught you in that class; just go out and kick ass." Case closed!

6. *Noncash reward systems that reward combativeness.* At one company I worked for, the people who screamed and whined the loudest got the perks—not necessarily the biggest bonuses (although that happened, too), but the best offices, the great trips, the choice assignments. Admittedly, some of these individuals did bring in exemplary results, but they forgot they were part of a team. Whenever they screamed, management rolled over. What was the unspoken message to the rest of us? "To get what you want, you have to be an uncooperative narcissist!"

7. *Frustrated managers/business owners who don't know how to regulate their anger.* A coaching client of mine, a really wonderful guy, had been called to the carpet for berating and demeaning his employees. When I met with him, he told me about his church and his family with tears in his eyes. But he was extraordinarily frustrated with the manufacturing process at work: people weren't doing what they were supposed to. His staff was struggling, and getting the blame for a lot of things that weren't their fault. Consequently, he regularly lost his cool. Although his anger and frustrations were justified, his outbursts were not, and without realizing it he was firing up conflict between his staff and other departments—quality control, R&D, engineering, and others. The point is, *just because he was right did not justify his actions.* Another

man I worked with, an entrepreneur, would frequently lose his temper and walk through the company. Whenever this happened, everyone would run for cover, trying to hide and avoid his wrath. The result? Productivity slipped. Here, too, this man's anger was justified, but not his actions.

8. *Company norms that don't encourage truth-telling.* You sit at a meeting and you know that 80 percent of what is being said is either not the truth or not what really needs to be said. So you sit there, looking at your watch, texting your buddy, or thinking of all the productive things you *could* be doing instead. You wish that someone would just tell it like it is for once, so the real issues could be addressed and you all could get on doing what you're supposed to be doing.

Just today I consulted with a small business owner who has two employees that are, as he described them, "lazy and not pulling their weight." I asked why they were still employed at the firm. The answer? No one had the heart (or guts) to fire them. Believe it or not, the owner was "hoping" these troublesome employees would one day wake up on their own so that he could avoid having to face a sticky situation. In a small company, where resources are especially critical, anyone not pulling his or her weight becomes an albatross around everyone else's neck. And if no one speaks the truth about employees not pulling their own weight, they will have no idea that they are failing.

Meanwhile, understandably, the other employees resented the two underperformers, who caused them to bear heavier workloads. More gasoline being poured on the flames of conflict! I don't need to paint the picture in any greater detail, do I?

Another example of the damage not telling the truth can do is the company or division where no one tells the boss the truth. What's really going on? He or she exists in a filtered cloud of information, and thus makes decisions that either hurt the business or foment conflict, or both.

9. *Blaming behavior and responsibility avoidance.* You've seen this, I am sure: A mistake happens at work and no one claims responsibility. Just the opposite, in fact: everyone scurries around trying to avoid blame. You ask someone what happened and he or she points to someone else. That kind of behavior fuels the flames of conflict and mistrust. I call this one the "blame game." When I first observed it, I asked my manager (with the naïveté of a young professional) why many senior people acted in such an irresponsible manner. His response sticks in my head to this day: "Because they have more at stake." It seemed to me that having more at stake would lead one to be impeccably responsible, but my boss chalked up my opinion to inexperience.

Keep in mind that the higher up you go on the corporate ladder, the more ripples your actions create. I still can't fathom why leaders allow themselves to behave as if avoiding responsibility will help them or the organization. What do you think? Isn't that exactly why we have so little trust in the people we elect?

At the lower end of the organizational chart, blaming behavior often flourishes. So much time gets wasted as a result; it is immeasurable.

10. *Just plain pains in the butt!* These are people who cause problems no matter where they go. We need to immunize against them! You have met many of them, no doubt; we all have. They are the topic of conversation/gossip in the

cafeteria; they are the butt of jokes. When I work in groups with someone like this in them, it seems no one knows quite how to deal with them. Enter The Working Circle!

Understanding where conflict comes from, how it arises, can help you to better deal with it. Recognizing and being able to characterize the different kinds of people who typically cause conflict is another invaluable tool.

Coworkers Who Instigate Conflict

We've all had experience with people who drive us crazy at work for one reason or another. Often, the conflict we have with them affects us personally—we report to a boss who doesn't know how to manage disagreements, or must collaborate with a colleague whose inability or unwillingness to carry his or her own weight affects our performance.

Let's take a look at the behavior of some troublesome types of coworkers—what it is about them that incites conflict—and then consider typical ways that organizations and people attempt to address and deal with these individuals. The usual methods generally are ineffective in resolving the conflicts they generate and, over time, the instigators end up with too much power and influence.

The Pot-Stirrer

I'll begin by describing the type I refer to as the "pot-stirrer," using as an example a receptionist at a company I worked for. This woman was delightful in many ways. She had a wonderful English accent. My office was down the hall from reception, and when my door was open, I could hear her as she answered the phone repeatedly during the day—not because she was loud, but because the office had an open-space design.

This receptionist was, however, a pot-stirrer. She would gossip all day, telling various people stories she had picked up or heard from someone else. Consequently, she was a source for much office intrigue. She would often tell one person what someone else had said about him or her. Gossip of this nature is one of the longstanding wellsprings of conflict. How many times have I become incensed after someone told me something that someone else said about me? Too many times to count! Most of the time, this really isn't useful information, and it often isn't accurate. Rather, the source of the information typically has some agenda he or she is working. Even if the source is a friend, the information is just that: information. These days, if someone tells me something that another person said about me, I just say, "Thank you," and move on. I also have made it a practice never to do that to anyone else. This kind of information gathering rarely, if ever, helps. On the contrary, it stirs the pot.

The Loner

Bill, a peer of mine, was so insecure that he insisted on making every decision himself. Working with him was an experience in constantly feeling shut out. My role was to collaborate with him on various initiatives, yet he never wanted to meet or work together. Instead, I would get missives about what he had done and what he had accomplished.

The loner functions only for himself and his progress, and is usually deaf to the ideas of others—unless of course those ideas come from the boss or the loner. People working with loners often go home feeling unheard, unsatisfied, and, so, frustrated.

There's another factor that comes into play when you make decisions only for yourself, versus joining with others to meet a common objective: it's called creativity. Creativity at work should not be an accident; It should be encouraged as part of the culture.

Having a vision requires the ability to take a clear, balanced look at the past, present, and future, and factor all of these into our final plan of action. However, because we are so busy, our lives are so fast-paced and so focused on what's going on today, we often ignore these steps of balanced thinking completely. As a result, short-term thinking can result in decision making that brings short-term, rather than long-term, results.

The Pleaser

When managers or employees want to be liked, you'll often see them contributing, offering ideas; they are always willing to put in their two cents. While on the surface this appears to be a collaborative approach, there can be a definite downside to it: they may just be telling the boss what he or she wants to hear. And if this happens often enough, you'll find that those individuals can't be trusted to think independently at all. In high school, we called this "brownnosing."

Many managers have told me that they don't want independent thinkers on their staffs; rather, they want the people who work for them to toe the line. These same managers are those who can't be away from the office because, "No one here can make a decision besides me!" Be careful what you ask for!

The pleaser doesn't make decisions; he or she just mimics what the boss wants. Those who want to think independently and contribute intelligence to the conversation start to resent the pleaser. Mistrust begins to grow, and that fuels the fires of conflict.

Most people justifiably see the pleaser as weak and unable to make decisions without help. This is obviously not a management profile that bodes well, either for individual or group success. Colleagues usually find themselves working around pleasers, thereby avoiding conflict and disempowering them. As a result, the team is seriously weakened.

If the pleaser is a team member, and the boss has a healthy level of self-confidence, the boss sees right through the pleaser's actions. Conversely, if the boss has low self-esteem and enjoys the constant affirmations from the pleaser, the team resents the pleaser even more. Either way, he or she causes conflict and mistrust. Some team members will feed the pleaser information that they want to filter to the boss. This breeds an environment marked by intense manipulation and abiding mistrust.

The Know-it-all

The flip side of the pleaser is the person who wants to shine, to stand out, even if it's at everyone else's expense. Take Dick, a manager who was offered a rather quick and substantial promotion in another division of his company. He was on the fast track and wanted to stay there: no one was going to stand in his way. At every meeting, with peers as well as staff, he had the answer to every question, had the data that no one else had. This was the case even if his answers weren't exactly factual. He was a challenge to work with.

Whenever Dick had made a decision, he would tell his confidants what he wanted to do and how wise his decision was. He would whisper that senior management was aligned with him (whether this was true or not), so all his confidants could do was agree with him. They knew there was no point in expressing their concerns or opinions, as Dick didn't really want to hear them.

Six months after Dick began his new job, people began transferring out of the division, and the rumor mill was rife with negative stories about him.

Watch out for that rumor mill—it is speedier and more effective than an organizationwide announcement!

The Chosen One

This type is one that always makes me laugh (if not out loud, at least to myself). The chosen one is the professional who thinks that the sun rises and sets on him or her. Everything good that happens is a result of his or her actions, inputs, or ideas. The word "we" is not in their lexicon. The chosen ones intimate either directly or indirectly that they have the ear of senior management. Their message to you suggests that you need to follow them if you want to succeed.

Believing that someone might be a chosen one makes it hard to deal with the conflict he or she stirs up. So what people often do is to wait in the bushes for the chosen one to slip and tumble. That might be an effective conflict strategy, but it also might backfire. People blindly jump on the band-wagon, ignore the chosen one, or undermine him or her. None of these machinations are good for the establishment!

The Wet Blanket

I am sure that you have met this person many, many times. No matter what you or anyone else says, wet blankets have something negative to say in response. No matter how good an idea might be, they have something critical to say about it. Personally, when I'm in a less than collaborative mood, I want to wring their necks! (Of course, with a doctorate in conflict resolution, I don't do it. But the mental image is quite delightful.)

If given too much power and/or credence, wet blankets take the air out of any discussion. But what usually happens is that they are challenged, and an argument ensues. The argument is either on the table or subterranean—more political maneuvering to undermine the wet blanket. This takes the focus away from the issue at hand, ticks people off, and leaves them less able to effectively problem solve.

I remember one particular scene: Connor, a team leader, was listening to differing opinions about his team and his management style. He wanted to get to the bottom of his issues so he could improve his style and motivate his team. He proposed a solution for one issue, and then asked for the staff's reactions and ideas.

Sue, a long-time associate, said, "Hey, Connor, remember when we tried something like this four years ago? It was a bad idea then and it won't work now."

After Sue said that, the room went quiet. She was viewed as negative, and so disregarded. When that happened, she became more negative still, further eroding team cohesion. Sue was stuck in the past, and rather than learning from it, she used it as her reason to remain negative. Her wet blanket behavior effectively shut down constructive conversation.

Fortunately, The Working Circle can be a highly effective means of moving wet blankets into a more promising future by showing them how focusing on how the past can be a source of learning, and bring positive results. This enables them to move ahead with confidence, and avoid blaming others for past mistakes.

The "My Porridge Is Too Hot" Client

We've all had interactions with these people, and maybe have actually behaved like this ourselves from time to time. (I certainly have, especially when I'm angry for being put on hold for an interminable amount of time!)

This client type is never satisfied, no matter what you do, no matter how hard you try. He or she has little patience, and prefers to accuse, rather than engage in a reasoned debate or discussion of options. If there is a cursory discussion, this person will dismiss suggestions from others almost as soon as they're uttered, or present a cold shoulder to any who counters his or her ideas. They are a particular challenge because they are customers/clients.

Clients like this can ruin your day. Many of us find ourselves intimidated, put off by this type, and would rather avoid them than deal with them. An employee who is seen as challenging this type of client may be accused of failing to be customer-oriented, and ends up even more frustrated than before. Ever find yourself in that situation?

"I've Got an Excuse for Everything" Worker

Many years ago I taught fifth grade in Brooklyn, New York. There were kids who didn't do their homework, didn't bring in forms that required parental signatures, and on and on. They always had an excuse; some were reasonable, some were outlandish. When I went into the corporate world, I saw what these children looked like when they became adults. Oh my!

Meeting deadlines is important, and doing so is particularly important to me. I remember Tom, who worked for me in Chicago. He was consistently late meeting assigned deadlines. His excuses were, at the beginning, understandable, especially when they had to do with his health. But then the excuses got more and more peculiar, as he couldn't keep repeating the same ones. I had to stifle my laughter, because the projects his lateness was interfering with were important, and I didn't want to undermine the seriousness of the situation.

These people can also be infuriating, as they hurt themselves and the team. One day, when I was out of town, Tom stormed out of the office, never to be seen again. My demands and his excuses had done him in!

The Whiner

I remember seeing a comic strip many years ago that stuck in my head. It was a drawing of a group of customers sitting at a bar, one of which was a donkey (or as we also say, an ass). The caption underneath the drawing read, "There's always one at every bar!" That's how I relate to the whiner.

If there is a bonus, the bonus isn't enough. If there is a new project, it is too difficult, and takes time away from other projects. If a new employee joins the team, he or she is not as good as the previous employee. You get the picture. Whiners suck the energy out of a team, leaving a vacuum that commonly gets filled with tension and conflict—the tension built off of the exasperation of others.

Very often, coworkers and managers try to assuage the whiner, which only leads to more whining. These people are perpetual downers who contribute little of value to the team's well-being and productivity.

Bosses Who Cause or Exacerbate Conflict

The higher up you go on the corporate ladder, the greater impact you have on the way conflict originates and is handled at the company. Here are some examples of management styles that make life much more difficult for the rest of the employees.

The Well-Meaning Gossip

Sandy, one of my former managers, was a well-meaning, intelligent woman who was unable to have a cohesive team. The reason is that she would talk about each of us to our peers, and then tell each of us what the others said (positive and negative) about us. Unwittingly, she was setting us up to be combative and uncooperative. When a team is like that, its members withhold critical information from one another in order to maintain the upper hand.

Another manager I knew would join staff members in maligning a certain individual on the team, usually the outcast. Jokes would be made at the outcast's expense, with the manager often participating. The outcast, over time, of course became totally disenfranchised and disempowered. Why have someone on the team who has no effectiveness?

Managers who set their team members against each other have teams that could be much more productive than they are. Their unconscious (and sometimes conscious) untrustworthy behavior makes it a real challenge to be collaborative with one's peers. The result is that team members are at each other's throats, and often don't know the real reason—the boss!

The "My Way or the Highway" Boss

Tony, who was head of collections at a Fortune 50 company, had a powerful personality. He stood about 6'2", and was not a lightweight. The first time I attended a management meeting that he convened, I was startled to see that no one would speak without first glancing at him. Even if the person was addressing someone else, he or she checked in with Tony as if to confirm that what he or she was saying was okay with him. And everyone knew when what they said was *not* okay: Tony glared and motioned with a hand to move on. It was a daunting experience to be the presenter (which I was) at one of those meetings!

I recall once asking for input on a human resources initiative I was working on at this company. One by one, each of Tony's managers made negative, unsupportive comments about my project. I was young then, and easily deflated. After the meeting, one of my peers in HR told me he had been in the men's room earlier, and had heard Tony talking to two of his managers (he had a total of nine).

"Tony instructed them to reject your project," my friend said. I was, in my naïveté, shocked and crushed. But I also learned something important, and subsequently developed a new strategy to deal with Tony, one that didn't include seeking input from his managers. Instead, he and I went head to head, with me attempting to meet his objections. I did make some progress—and, as I said, learned some lessons about this kind of manager.

Tony was successful for a long time, but his style ultimately became his downfall. He was retired a few years later.

The Moody Manager

When this type of manager is, "on," the place just hums. Everyone is productive and the stress level comes down. But when this boss goes "off," everyone runs to their offices or cubicles. Many small business owners are like this, though this type certainly isn't limited to small organizations. The moody manager runs hot and cold, according to his or her moods, fears, or level of excitement. Such individuals don't understand the impact their moods and actions have on others.

I have also witnessed small business owners who share their fears with their employees, which generally get magnified by the employees. And, as we all know, fear can bring out negative behavior. At the very least, it slows productivity. That negative behavior can also bring about conflict, conflict that these leaders aren't capable of handling because they are trapped by their own fear. Organizations then become either stalled or internally driven, instead of market driven.

When the moody manager is on, he or she prances around the office telling jokes or stories of their successes. This behavior has less of a negative impact on the staff, as the good mood is contagious. It is when the switch goes off that conflict and upset arise, distracting employees from the business at hand.

We have all seen television shows and movies that depict office workers gearing themselves up for the entrance of the moody manager. Everyone holds their breath until they determine which mood the boss is in, and what that will mean for their workday. It is the manager's job to build motivation and invoke a positive mood among the staff, not to impose his or her bad mood on everyone else.

The Boss Who Can't Delegate

"Why should I delegate? It will take less time to do it myself!"

This is the boss whose inbox is a mile high, who is always stressed, and who slows things down because he or she is always overworked. This results in chaos, a team lacking discipline, and confusion. Chaos is a powerful fuel for conflict, due to mixed signals, unclear accountabilities, and stalled decision making. This boss hoards work (with good intentions, most of the time), forcing the staff to go to him or her before making even the smallest decisions.

Bosses who can't, or won't, delegate real responsibility, only know how to assign tasks. A staff that does not have decision-making power can only contribute dribs and drabs to the business. They become a bunch of doers, without also being thinkers. What eventually happens is, they start fighting over the few morsels of power that might be on the horizon. This conflict then leads the boss to believe that he or she is correct in not giving them decision-making power. It is a vicious cycle: the business produces more automatons, while the boss grows old at a very young age.

Summary

Those are some of the ways to, and some of the people who, fuel conflict in organizations. It doesn't matter what kind of organization it is—a government agency, a for-profit business, or a nonprofit institution. Most of the time, the individuals described here are well-meaning. (Note that the list could have been much longer, but I chose the most prevalent ones, as well as those I work with most frequently using The Working Circle).

What, then, is the best way to handle business conflicts when they affect you and the success of your group? Enter The Working Circle! As demonstrated in the following pages, this approach will enable you to think things through (alone or as part of a team); incorporate a wide variety of factors and ideas; and examine the past, present, and future without disempowering anyone. In the end, both individuals and teams are strengthened, as everyone gets to play a positive role in reaching the best decisions and achieving success.

Chapter 2

The Working Circle's Eight Key Questions

When conflict needs to be resolved, decisions have to be made. There is so much juggling at work, with deadlines, personalities, and tasks, that conflict resolution should be as easy as possible. If the underlying issues aren't addressed, the same type of conflict will keep coming up over and over again. As discussed in Chapter 1, logic is a cornerstone of decision making; just as important is that ephemeral quality, *intuition*. The Working Circle incorporates both approaches, to help professionals at any level arrive at balanced decisions with confidence.

Naturally, we will begin with Question 1. As we progress around the circle, we can go back and forth, as needed. Notice in the diagram of The Working Circle that Question 1 begins on the right-hand, or east, side. The east is where the sun rises. With the rising sun comes the emergence of perspectives, creativity, and questions. Directionally, the east is the place of beginnings and *orientation*. When you begin a new job, you may be given an orientation (at least, you should be!).

Creativity is an essential aspect of decision making. While we need to gather data and facts, we also need to search our hearts and histories to find creative solutions to life's dilemmas. When data and intuition are united, we can resolve career dilemmas with greater intelligence, depth, and even panache. A critical aspect of the Circle, as I explained in Chapter 1, is the balance between the masculine left brain and the feminine right brain. I can't overemphasize this point.

I have worked with engineering firms where, understandably, left-brain capabilities are highly valued. Any emotional component to decision making is usually ignored. It is not surprising then that conflicts are treated as annoyances; they get in the way, so are often sidestepped. In one engineering firm, where innovation is touted, the staff loses a great deal by avoiding conflicts and ignoring their intuition.

In contrast, when I worked with a successful spa, where creativity and emotionalism were allowed to run rampant, they talked issues to death and often ended up where they started! They sidestepped analysis and were overconcerned with the emotional, and so they lost the left-brained approach to decision making, as well.

Let's now look at an example that has affected us all: the economic crash that occurred in September 2008. Almost immediately, the media and members of the government vigorously engaged in the blame game. This is a commonly played game that you have experienced over and over again, I am certain. Who was to blame, who was at fault, whose ideas were wrong, who was evil, and so on, ad nauseam. There was no nonpartisan discussion of, *What can we learn from this?*

The masculine side zooms to the attack, when what we need is acknowledgment of responsibility and a desire to learn from the situation. That acknowledgment is very different from blame. By adding the feminine perspective of the situation, we would ask, "What alliances can we build for the good of all?" that would have modified the usual Washington polarization.

A reminder: When I refer to masculine and feminine, I am not referring to men and women, per se, rather the typical approach of the genders, not all or specific individuals.

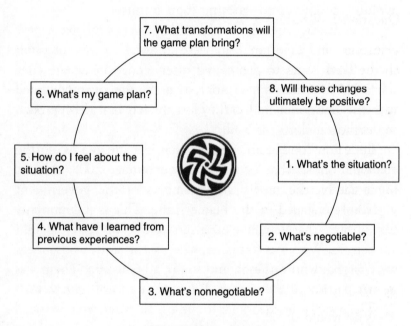

The Working Circle

As you now enter The Working Circle, you can (whether you have been more reliant on the left or the right side of your brain) now begin to resolve conflict in a balanced manner.

To illustrate this, let's travel through The Working Circle step by step, to see how it's set up to work for you.

Question 1: What's the Situation?

Question 1 urges you to look at your situation clearly, focusing on the facts. What exactly is going on?

To do this, first, put all your emotions and opinions aside and consider the facts only. Think of yourself as a camera, moving to all angles in turn and snapping the facts as images of the situation. You'll record only the people, places, and things involved. Emotions, opinions, judgments, points of view are out of the picture; only hard facts prevail at this point.

Now let's look at a list of queries you might ask yourself to help answer Question 1:

- When did the situation begin?
- Who is involved?
- Who would be affected by the decisions made?
- What impact has the situation had on others?
- How has the situation affected you?
- What were the events leading up to the current situation?
- What happened that made the situation escalate?
- What brought about the need for change and/or resolution?
- Are there any time frames/deadlines involved that require a decision by a certain date?
- Who needs to be involved in the decision-making process?

We'll follow one woman's situation to highlight the process.

Kim was a senior associate at a consulting firm. She loved her work, and especially loved the travel involved. However, her colleague, Tony, (also a senior associate) with whom she often traveled, tended to intimidate her. When they sat together at client meetings, she would slowly shut down and let Tony take the lead. Tony gladly allowed this to take place, and eventually left Kim out of the discussion entirely. She'd sit there mutely as Tony ran with the project, wondering why she was even there.

In time the situation deteriorated further. Tony would delegate tasks to Kim that she found particularly demeaning. Finally, Kim decided that she had to do something about the situation and, putting her emotions aside, she began to examine the facts of the situation:

- Kim and Tony had been working together for one year.
- Tony had been at the firm one year longer than Kim.
- Tony was more analytical than Kim, but Kim had a greater capacity for problem solving with clients.
- Kim knew that if she did not address the situation, she would continue sending Tony the message that he was more skilled than she. He would then assume even more of a leadership role.
- Their manager, Brett, didn't meet with them often, and really didn't want to hear about any issues or problems they were having.

By dispassionately examining the situation in this way, Kim had answered Question 1 for herself.

It is important to be dispassionate and thorough when you begin to address Question 1—keep in mind the camera perspective.

Question 2: What's Negotiable?

Once you have a clear grasp of the situation, you can begin to determine what are both the important and noncritical components you need to solve your dilemma. Question 2 invites you to sift through the facts to identify what you're willing to negotiate, give away, or compromise in order to solve your problem.

Asking "what's negotiable?" is another way of saying, "I realize that not everything is critical to produce a successful result. To figure out what I want to do, I need to know which elements are vital to my perspective, and which are not. Being able to sort through all these possibilities will help me arrive more quickly at a game plan."

The questions to ask yourself, in order to answer what is negotiable, are:

- In this conflict, which aspects or items could I leave behind?
- Which contentious items am I willing to discuss and modify through negotiations?
- If pressed by my adversary, which items am I willing to let go of or change?
- How much of certain aspects of the conflict am I willing to settle for?

When Kim asked herself "what's negotiable?" she came up with this list of items:

● She was willing to share the lead with Tony in working with clients, as long as it ended up being 50/50.

● She agreed that either of them could take "credit" with their manager, again as long as the end result was a 50/50 split.

● She might not necessarily want to work with Tony as a partner. At the end of the fiscal year, when new assignments were made, she might ask to work with another peer.

Typically, when we first come face to face with crucial decisions, everything seems important. The situation seems to be the most important one we have ever been confronted with, and the options can be overwhelming. Asking "what's negotiable?" allows us to examine everything associated with the situation and determine what is and isn't crucial.

When Kim made a list of what was negotiable, she felt less overwhelmed. Once she knew what she could give up, she could move on to Question 3.

Question 3: What's Nonnegotiable?

On the other side of the equation, we need to also look at which items or aspects of the conflict are immutable. By asking ourselves what's nonnegotiable, we decide where we are not willing to budge, where we will stand fast and say, "No." It may be drawing a line at how we are being treated; it could be a dollar amount; it could be any item involved in the conflict. Whatever it is, we make a choice *not* to concede this item. In truth, Question 3 actually asks, "What are you willing to fight for?" That gets translated to, "What's nonnegotiable?"

Let's continue with our friend, Kim, who is now ready to ask herself, "What's nonnegotiable?"

Here's what she came up with:

- She needed to be the leader with clients half the time, and to have Tony take a back seat at those times.
- She refused to allow Tony take credit for her work.
- She wanted to share the workload, rather than have Tony delegate to her.
- She was willing to share some of the more odious tasks, as opposed to taking on all of them and, thus, freeing Tony from them.
- She wanted her clients, her manager, and Tony to regard, and treat, her and Tony as a team.

Kim vacillated between what was negotiable and what was nonnegotiable until she felt that she had a balanced-enough list to move to the next question. Going back and forth between Questions 2 and 3 allows for the development of more comprehensive answers to each.

Let's consider now what happens when more than one person has something at stake in the decision-making process. In this situation, each person should determine what he or she must have and what he or she is willing to give up to achieve the best end result.

For example, assume you tell your boss that taking Christmas week off to be with your kids is nonnegotiable: by making this clear, he or she knows where you stand and can plan for your absence should any future decision-making opportunities arise.

When I worked in corporate management, I considered meeting deadlines to be nonnegotiable. I expected my staff to either meet their deadlines or, well in advance of the deadline, come to me to explain why they couldn't and negotiate a new due date. Everyone who worked for me knew I did not want to have to remind them when their projects were due. They certainly knew where I stood, and in this way, I was able to deal efficiently with transgressions and never had to face any unpleasant surprises.

A manager, when dealing with his or her team, can ask what's negotiable and nonnegotiable in any situation. Included in the answer could be:

- Time frames
- Resources (money and things)
- Staff members
- Communication—frequency and/or method (phone, face to face, e-mail, etc.)
- Accountabilities (who does what)
- Standards of quality
- Documentation

The more we know about each other's critical and non-critical items, the less likely there will be any surprises later—as in, "Gee, I didn't know it was *that* important."

What's negotiable and nonnegotiable must be clearly stated and clearly defined. This means that you need to take a stand. Changing how someone has treated you in the past might be nonnegotiable, and you might need to state that clearly—for example, "It's not acceptable to expect me to work late on Fridays."

Once you are satisfied with your lists of both negotiable and nonnegotiable issues, you are ready to move on to the next question.

It really resonates with clients when I refer to Question 3 as the "What hill am I willing to die on?" question. Then I point out that it is in the South where the sun shines the brightest!

Question 4: What Have I Learned from Previous Experiences?

Using your past experiences as lessons to learn from, so that you can make better decisions in the present and future is, alas, something I rarely see happen in organizations. The mistakes of the past are usually bemoaned as experiences not to be repeated, yet there is rarely any discussion about how to ensure that those involved in these negative experiences have learned from their mistakes. Punishment may occur, but rarely conscious, organization-wide learning.

As Kim continued through The Working Circle, it was important that she keep in mind that it is counterproductive to be negative when problem solving. This is because:

- Past experience, even if unpleasant, can provide information for future growth.
- Past experience is valuable as long as it is communicated in a way that will advance the problem-solving process.

Question 4 reminds us that if we have been through similar situations relevant to the current impasse, sharing what we gained from those experiences can help others in their decision-making process.

Kim sat quietly for awhile as she contemplated Question 4. She remembered that when she was 16 years old, three girls in her gym class enjoyed harassing her in the locker room. Consequently, she began to dread attending gym class, and spent long hours fretting over what to do about it.

One day, as she was going into the locker room, she noticed that one of the bullies was standing alone. The other two girls were somewhere else, and the one remaining was bending down, apparently searching for something.

"Did you lose something?" Kim asked helpfully. Surprised, her nemesis looked up and said, "I lost my bracelet."

Kim sank down onto the floor and helped the girl search for her lost bracelet. "Here it is," she said a few minutes later, holding it up. She handed it to the other girl, who was clearly relieved and grateful.

"Thanks," she said very quietly to Kim. After that incident, the three girls didn't bother Kim again. At times they made mild jokes, but the harassment never had the same intensity as it had previously.

Now, sitting at her desk at work, Kim realized that she had learned a valuable lesson: to treat bullies as equals, rather than avoid them and give them the upper hand. She also learned the importance of behaving as a considerate human being, rather than emulating the bad behavior of the bullies.

Considering her past experience, Kim felt more confident about how she needed to behave with Tony, and so moved on to Question 5.

Very often, you'll find that your response to Question 4 reminds you of difficult situations you've been through before, that you came out of them whole, and may even have learned a thing or two that is helpful to you today. We also often tend to treat the current situation as absolutely the worst we have ever been through. Working through Question 4 reminds us we have faced multiple challenges, which empower us to deal with today's.

Question 5: How Do I Feel about the Situation?

Question 5 allows us to stop for a moment and ask ourselves how we feel. How we answer will revolve around the following issues:

● How we feel about the players in the situation.

- How we feel about our ability to make up a game plan (the next step in the process).
- How we feel about the information we have gathered—is it adequate?
- How we feel about our ability to proceed.
- Whether or not we might benefit from the outcome.

Think about it: When you need to make important decisions, aren't emotions present? When there is conflict, aren't emotions involved? And yet, how often will someone at a meeting ask, "Okay, but how do we really *feel* about moving forward?"

There are a couple of reasons why feelings aren't exposed during decision-making meetings:

- Fear that these feelings will set off a tsunami of emotion, blocking rational decision making.
- The sense that everyone is already aware the feelings are present and that they are self-evident. Usually, men make this assumption—yes, everyone is worried, so why talk about it? Women, on the other hand, might talk about emotions but not participate in a discussion of them to advance the decision-making process. Emotional conversation is not productive when it becomes a complaint session, rather than a clearing of blockages.

When was the last time you heard a rumor making the rounds in your organization? What feelings were evoked by these rumors? What impact did those fears, worries, and anxieties have on productivity? I'm willing to bet that those emotions slowed down the organization considerably. People were spending more time talking about impending doom than they did on their work. If we paid a bit more attention to how people were feeling, we could significantly improve productivity and morale.

Women generally have an easier time relating to emotions. However, at work, usually they can't appear to be soft or too touchy-feely. Working with emotions has to be *part* of the process, not an *end* to the process. A manager who tells his or her team not to worry only arouses more worry. Acknowledging worry goes a long way toward minimizing it. Facing the emotions inherent to any situation enables us to deal with them and move on.

Back to our friend, Kim, who had been intimidated by Tony, but now wants to tell him how she has felt in the past: consistently mistreated by him. However, she has no idea how to approach the situation. By using The Working Circle, she realized that she was no longer afraid to approach Tony, because she had tapped into her past experiences with bullies and, in doing so, now feels strong enough to devise a game plan for herself. Kim is confident that she has been thorough in answering Questions 1 through 5; in other words, she does not feel incomplete. Feeling incomplete can be a signal to go back to previous questions and consider them one more time.

Because Kim no longer fears a confrontation, she can now move on to Question 6, which will help her create the all-important game plan.

Question 6: What's My Game Plan?

This is probably the question you are most familiar with: What are you going to do? Answering it is the linear part of the process, when we make project plans, assign timelines, draw Gantt charts, and so on.

Point: The more complex a dilemma, the more complex the plans. So much has been written about project planning that I will not take up space in this book to deal with it. Suffice to say, we have arrived at the place of actual project planning.

Kim has decided that on her next business trip with Tony to a client site, she will discuss what has been concerning her. She now reviews the main points of her plan. She:

- Is determined not to confront Tony, but instead to maintain a friendly demeanor.
- Commits to standing firm until Tony understands that she considers them equals and work partners.
- Intends to clarify what she is uncomfortable discussing in front of clients, and which discussions she believes should take place in private.
- Does not try to anticipate what Tony will say. Instead, she plans what she wants to say and when she will say it.
- Decides she will use an upcoming project to discuss these issues, rather than rehashing the past, which could lead to defensiveness on Tony's part and ill will between them.
- Commits to be firm and professional, to maintain eye contact, and not accuse Tony of anything. She just wants to speak assertively on her own behalf.

Question 6 allows you, like Kim, to use all the information you have accumulated from the first five questions to help draw up your game plan.

With that plan completed, you're probably thinking you're finished with The Working Circle, right?

Well, not quite . . .

Question 7: What Transformations Will the Game Plan Bring?

When I'm guiding a client through The Working Circle and we finish with Question 6, the client often cheers, "Hooray, I'm finished!" When this happens, I smile and pretend to bar the door, then explain to the client about Question 7 and why it is so important.

Your planning process will be much richer and more likely to succeed if you project the consequences of your plan. That's the purpose of Question 7. It encourages you to begin living your plan. What are the positive benefits your plan might bring you? How would you like to be transformed as a result? Does this plan assure you of a positive transformation?

Question 7 is at the core of what is called *Transformational Conflict Resolution*. Not only do you want to resolve the issue, you want to learn from it as well, and implement change. This is critical if you don't want to keep repeating negative situations over and over again.

The different ways of approaching Question 7 are:

- How will you be changed by the outcome?
- How could your relationship with the other person(s) be changed?
- How could this impact your future?
- How could this improve your self-esteem?
- How could you alter your ability to deal with future conflict?

Let's see how Kim handled this step. After she completed her game plan, she sat back and reflected. If she was clear, assertive, and professional in her discussion with Tony, she could accomplish her goal of working with him as an equal. This would give her new self-confidence, enable her to be more relaxed with their clients, and bring her more respect from Tony, her other teammates, and her manager. Was that something she wanted? Absolutely!

But first, she has one final question to tackle.

Question 8: Will These Changes Ultimately Be Positive?

Question 8 provides you with that all-important final check before you actually initiate your plan. If you have been diligent in answering the first seven questions, you should be able to move rather briskly through this question. Let's see how Kim handles it.

She looks at the notes she has written while answering the first seven questions comprising The Working Circle. Would this new assertiveness be good for her future? Without doubt! She can see herself leaving meetings without feeling bad because she had not stood up for herself. She also imagines how much more comfortable she will become with her superiors at work. This increased comfort level could, she knows, leads to greater recognition for her achievements.

I learned long ago that if you put your *intention* where you want to go, your *attention* will follow. If you focus on the changes you would like to see take place as a result of your efforts, they're far more likely to occur. One of my clients was able to win the job she had been wanting by spending 10 minutes a day observing herself going through the motions of a typical day on the new job. She saw herself smoothly handling any issues that arose. She even saw the outfit she'd be wearing when the job was offered to her! Sure enough, to everyone else's surprise, she won the job, and the other top candidate was unexpectedly given a lateral transfer.

Question 8 will motivate you to look at the future. Of course, none of us can predict the future, but we certainly can be better prepared for it by focusing on potential results and consequences, both positive and negative.

If more corporations would look at Question 8 in greater depth, they would produce stronger long-term results. The future extends further than the next quarter—it goes well beyond that! Had more organizations done that in the recent past, the devastating credit bomb that exploded in 2008 would not have been nearly so damaging.

Making decisions is not easy. They typically involve complex issues, emotions, and long-standing situations that are difficult to resolve. No one teaches us *how* to make decisions; from childhood, we are *told* what decisions to make. Using The Working Circle process, a both flexible and comprehensive process, you can learn the skills you need to face your career challenges and conflicts with ease and thoughtfulness. The more you use The Working Circle process, the more comfortable and confident you will become, making it easier to select the appropriate questions to ask to address each new situation.

Now we're ready to explore how The Working Circle can take you to the Winner's Circle—every single time!

PART TWO

UNDERSTANDING CONFLICT RESOLUTION

Chapter 3

What's Your Conflict Resolution Style?

Like most of us, I learned how to deal with conflict (rather ineffectively, I might add) at home when I was a kid. In my house, we yelled when we were angry, and I cried when I got upset. Going to work, the unwritten rules I learned were that you did not yell or cry. (I subsequently learned that losing your temper was acceptable if you were a prima donna or a bully with clout.)

I picked up such cues everywhere I worked, learning as I went along what the accepted conflict behavior was at each job I held. On Wall Street, raising one's voice and being confrontational were often the norms. When I moved to Tucson, by contrast, I learned that not disagreeing openly, and smiling and doing what you wanted to do is the norm.

Of course, I am exaggerating somewhat here, but you get my point. Every organization has a conflict resolution culture: its norms of behavior and unwritten rules about how conflict is and is not handled.

In some company cultures, no one deals directly with conflict; it is discussed with others not involved. Confrontation, even in a problem-solving manner, is viewed as impolite. In other cultures, it is more acceptable to complain to your allies and not address your adversaries. Other businesses follow the custom that allows for some confrontation and some undermining of one's adversaries. And, finally, there are those organizations that encourage problem-solving processes, and even offer confidential mediation.

Like organizations, individuals, too, have a personal way of dealing with conflict. For the participants in my "Conflict Resolution for Professionals" seminar, I developed a Conflict Styles Questionnaire. It has turned out to be quite reliable, based on empirical reporting of more than 1,500 professionals (I have never done a formal statistical evaluation). I provide it here so that you can take it to determine your conflict resolution style.

I am confident that you will find knowing how you handle conflict to be a great help to you both personally and professionally; for once you do, you will be able to see in which direction you need to move to become more of a problem solver and less of a problem maker. One of the most common remarks I hear when teaching is, "I hate conflict; I am so uncomfortable with it." Sound familiar? Well, let me reassure you that you *do not have to learn how to confront.* This usually is people's greatest fear. What they need is The Working Circle.

But before I take you through The Working Circle, I ask you to complete the questionnaire and see how the results compare with the view you currently have of yourself in this regard. Armed with this self-knowledge and The Working Circle, I assure you, you will be able to resolve issues in a much more effective way than you ever have before!

Conflict Management Style Questionnaire

Directions

For the following scenarios, using the legend below as a guide, choose a number that best describes how you would most likely handle that situation, and insert it in the box in the right-hand column of the table. When you're done, total the points for all of your responses.

1. You're really angry, and you're not going to take it anymore! You corner the other person, and without any preliminary discussion, let him or her know how you feel.

2. You deal with the person straight on, and directly identify the issues, leaving no room for give and take.

3. You approach the person as an equal and work the issues through collaboratively.

4. You give in to the other person's desires or demands. It's not exactly what you want, but you take this route to avoid further conflict.

5. You think about what you would say, but you usually avoid confronting others. You talk to friends or allies about the situation but not the person involved.

Scoring the Conflict Style Questionnaire

Directions   Compare your overall score from the questionnaire to the score ranges in the table here. After you find your score range, look to the right of that range to identify your conflict management style of. Then read the consequences of practicing your style of conflict management in the following sections.

Score	Style
10–23	Attacking/Confronting
24–37	Problem Solving
38–50	Compromising/Withdrawing

Conflict Styles Questionnaire

1.	Your peer recently took credit for work that you did, and now you are at lunch with him.	
2.	Your manager is four months late conducting your review, and tells you to please wait another two months.	
3.	You get an e-mail from a staff member telling you that you are playing favorites.	
4.	The IT technician told you that your system will be down for two days due to his not having received instructions that you said you sent him.	
5.	A friend of yours at work told you that a member of your unit has been negative and highly critical of you behind your back.	
6.	A vendor called to tell you that the items you ordered for your manager will arrive two weeks later than promised. This is the third time that this has happened.	
7.	A client waiting to see your manager tells you that every time she has met with him, he has been late, and if she has to wait any longer, she is canceling the contract.	
8.	Another supervisor has consistently provided incorrect information when you requested data, and did it again today.	
9.	A new member of your team has lied about his excessive absences, which were in fact due to going out of town for pleasure rather than illness.	
10.	You receive a memo from your manager saying that she thinks your unit is not performing up to par. She often jumps to conclusions, and this assessment is erroneous.	
	Total:	

Conflict Management Styles

Attacking   With this style, there are angry accusations; no real problem solving is going on. It is an opportunity for the attacker to ventilate, not solve problems.

Confronting   If you are confrontational, you deal with the person straight on, and directly identify the issues, but you don't allow for any give and take. Finding fault is more important to you than resolving any issues and/or learning anything from the experience.

Problem Solving   You approach the person you're in conflict with as an equal and work through your issues collaboratively. Emotions may be expressed, yes, but blame is not the goal; accountability is. Learning new behavior is possible.

Compromising   You give in to the other person's desires or demands. It's not exactly what you want, but you take this route to avoid further conflict. Even though you can learn new behavior and express how you feel, you walk away feeling shortchanged more often than not.

Withdrawing   When facing a conflict, you think about what you would like to say, but you usually avoid confronting others. Instead, you complain to friends or other colleagues about the situation, but not to the person involved. When you go to bed at night, inevitably you think of all the things you could/should have said. Conflict really makes you uncomfortable.

Consequences of Conflict Management Styles

Attacking   Some might tell you what they think you want to hear; others may feel alienated and perceive that they are never given an opening to talk to you. This style shuts others down, causing them either to withdraw or attack back. Creative problem solving is not an option.

Confronting   The person you confront becomes defensive, or argues with you to prove his or her point or demonstrate innocence. He or she may feel put on the spot, surprised, or alienated. People know you don't mince words. This style allows for minimal creativity in problem solving; rather, fault finding is the norm.

Problem Solving   People who are problem solvers make others feel included and valued. This is generally viewed as a win-win approach. When people deal with problem solvers, they feel that creativity is encouraged and rewarded, as in an open exchange of ideas. Even disagreement is treated as an opportunity for creative problem solving.

Compromising   Compromise is an effective tool in conflict management; it allows for a win-win approach. If, however, you use compromise as the predominant way to resolve conflict, you may be viewed as too nice, or even wishy-washy; others may feel that they can manipulate you. You may come away from a conflict resolution session feeling as though you didn't get what you really wanted. Compromise does offer some chance for creativity in addressing conflict.

Withdrawing   If you typically withdraw in the face of conflict, no one will know what is important to you or when something has upset you. And you feel as though your needs go unmet. People may note your absence but not understand why you have withdrawn. Withdrawing does not allow for creative problem solving, and issues may never get resolved. You have a lot of should have/could have thoughts.

Variables Regarding Conflict Management Styles

Attacking   This is a style that rarely is necessary or helpful in problem solving. Extreme anger or intense intimidation accompanies this style. In practice, this style may be effective in the short term, but does not work long term.

Confronting   When there are no options to discuss, this is a style that can work. Confronting generally means meeting face to face. In American culture, "in your face" is the colloquial term used for being confrontational. In certain circumstances, confronting someone is the only way that your opponent will listen. But after getting someone's attention, it helps to then switch to the problem-solving style.

Problem Solving   This is the optimal style, useful for eliciting creativity, empowerment, and mutual respect. Thus, it is the style supported by The Working Circle. It can be used even in highly charged situations, where the stakes are high and the conflict is a long-standing one.

Compromising   For the compromising style to be effective, each side needs to be willing to give in a little. It is a productive method when the stakes are not very high or one side has a greater investment in the outcome than the other. The downside to is that you might walk away without that win-win feeling if you were the one doing most of the compromising.

Withdrawing   You may withdraw from conflict when it is not important to you to become embroiled, when you are highly intimidated by your adversary, or you are simply afraid of conflict. So, you say nothing. For those who withdraw, conflicts don't get resolved, resentment can grow, and situations can even get worse. This is especially true if the conflict revolves around important issues.

Styles Summary

So many people equate conflict resolution with being confrontational. This is not the case! Confronting is what took place in my childhood home in Brooklyn. ("Who ate the cookies?!") It's what I see at many corporations. ("Who screwed up?!") It's what you hear in the news, from opinionated talking heads representing either side of the spectrum.

Many participants of my seminars will say at the beginning, "I am so uncomfortable with conflict. I hate confronting!" By the end of the class, however, they have achieved a much higher level of comfort because they have been given a process to follow, and they realize that resolving conflict does *not* have to involve confrontation!

Other participants will announce, "I'm here because my manager sent me, but I think this is a load of crap!" Welcome to class! I smile, recognizing that before me is a professional who enjoys conflict, and confronts others regularly. They are a far greater challenge to work with because they tend to reject the balanced, masculine/feminine approach to conflict resolution. Those who do adopt The Working Circle, however, learn to develop better working relationships, and find that more people want to cooperate with them.

Knowing your Conflict Resolution Style will help you in various ways:

- Self-knowledge can lead to self improvement.
- If you see that your current style is getting you into trouble, you can start to shift to another.

- ● You can better understand the styles of other people, leading you deal to more effectively with them.
- ● You can learn how and when to use a variety of styles, depending on the situation and your level of comfort.

Applying Conflict Resolution Style to The Working Circle

The range of styles can be superimposed on a continuum.

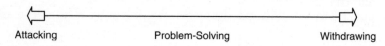

Attacking   Problem-Solving   Withdrawing

Traditionally in our culture, the attacking style is seen as a masculine trait, and the withdrawing style as a feminine trait. This in not to say that only men attack or only women withdraw. I am sure you can come up with numerous examples of men and women who act in ways that are not gender-specific.

Because The Working Circle balances masculine and feminine approaches to conflict resolution, we can them superimpose the masculine and feminine traits on the conflict style continuum, as shown here.

Masculine-Feminine Continuum

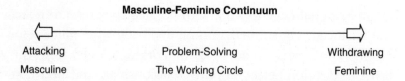

Attacking   Problem-Solving   Withdrawing
Masculine   The Working Circle   Feminine

Doing too much of anything is rarely a good thing. Sometimes it is advisable to withdraw (e.g., the boss who threatens to fire you when you are not ready to leave). Sometimes, though infrequently, it is advisable to attack (enter the market before a competitor does). With The Working Circle, we want to learn to use the problem-solving approach as much as we can, relying on neither the masculine nor feminine approach too often.

In the next chapter, I will describe eight different classic situations that occur in most people's careers at one time or another. For each, I will highlight the traditional masculine and feminine approaches, and then use The Working Circle to achieve a balanced, problem-solving tactic. I am confident that the more you use the balanced style, the greater your chances of becoming a winner—and enabling others to win with you.

Note: Please feel free to use the Conflict Resolution Questionnaire with coworkers, friends, and family. If you do, I'd love to hear from you about how it worked.

PART THREE

FROM THE WORKING CIRCLE TO THE WINNER'S CIRCLE

FROM THE WORKING CIRCLE TO THE WINNER'S CIRCLE

Eight Challenges, Eight Decisions

Part III comprises eight chapters in which I describe, in turn, eight situations that many people find themselves in at various times in their careers. The first one, about money, is generic, as we all have to face challenges and conflicts involving money. The subsequent seven are actual situations I have come across in my travels. The characters are real people, as are their stories— although the names and details have, of course, been changed to protect the privacy of the organizations and individuals involved.

As I described previously, The Working Circle incorporates both the masculine and feminine approaches to conflict, so for each of the eight challenges, I will highlight the spectrum of stereotypical masculine and feminine responses, on what I call the *Masculine-Feminine Continuum*. As you read, I will explain how The Working Circle can provide you with a process for reaching a balanced approach for each situation, and how it can serve as a tool enabling you to determine which is the most balanced and comfortable approach for you, regardless of your conflict resolution style.

I describe the typical responses as masculine and feminine. This in no way limits masculine responses to men, or feminine responses to women. I know lots of men who initiate conflict resolution with a feminine response, and women who characteristically take a more masculine approach to conflict resolution. The Working Circle is about balancing your style, no matter what your gender.

Chapter 4

Challenge 1

Ask Your Manager for the Raise You Deserve or "Be Happy You Have a Job"?

At some time (if not many times) in everyone's career, there is a discussion, a request, or a negotiation surrounding getting paid. For some of us, dealing with this issue comes easy; for others, it's agony. Either way, we need to be able to determine what we are worth, and know how to seek and receive it.

I believe salary increases should be earned—that is, they shouldn't just be given because it's time. I also believe that employees should not have to ask for raises; employers should initiate the process.

Compensation is a very hot topic currently, fueled by Wall Street pay practices, government intervention, and public anger. I first heard the term "golden handcuffs" in the 1980s: People who had a critical book of business or a particular skill set were compensated in such a way as to keep them tied to the company. There was often a boomerang effect, however: the handcuffed individuals kept asking for more and more, with the result that even in hard times, certain individuals continued to be extravagantly compensated, causing others to resent them and the company. That resentment fed discontent and caused further erosion of loyalty between employer and employee.

During up-cycles, when revenue is rolling in, compensation is a very different topic than during times of contraction. It seems, on some levels, that you work harder during lean times and get fewer rewards. I can't tell you how many times I've heard a manager tell an employee, "You should be happy you have a job." What wasn't said quite as often was, "And we're lucky to have you, and we appreciate the great job you do."

At least in part, we go to work to earn money, and it is one of the most difficult and sensitive topics to discuss fairly and openly, for both managers and employees. To begin to address this challenge, I'll introduce a situation that most of us are familiar with: asking for what we believe is fair compensation for the work we do.

Assume here that because of circumstances, you have to be the initiator of the conversation—if you don't do it, you fear no one else will. It could be there is no system in place to remind managers to conduct salary reviews; it could be there's no money for raises this year, or it could be that your boss is concerned about his or her raise, not yours. Whatever the reason, your patience has worn thin.

You've worked hard. You know that other people have gotten what they asked for; and some didn't even have to ask, you are sure. To make matters worse, according to the rumor mill, the jerk next to you just got a big salary hike. He is certainly acting like the star of the show lately. You're too nice and work too hard, you think. It's time to make more money, but you don't want to leave the company—now isn't the time. However, your boss never seems to be available for this kind of discussion, and, truth be told, you never feel quite ready for it either. You wish management would just do what they're supposed to do and give you that bonus and that raise! You know you have to do or say something, or you will just become more and more angry and resentful—not what you want at all!

Enter The Working Circle

Time to go to The Working Circle and answer the eight questions in turn.

Question 1: What's the Situation?

Reminder: This is when you analyze the situation, examining it without bias or opinion. To answer Question 1, remember, you start by acting like a camera, snapping facts that surround the dilemma. For Challenge 1, we'll assume these are the facts:

- Your last raise was two years ago.
- You've been working at the company for three years.
- You haven't had a salary review in two years.
- Your friend in another department told you that he is getting a raise—minimal, but a raise nonetheless.
- You're doing a good job—well, at least no one has told you you're not. (That's how feedback works at your company!)
- Your boss won't stay on topic when you try to talk to her; whenever you approach her, she gets distracted—by the phone, IMs, other interruptions.
- The project you just finished was very well received by the senior team.
- Your living expenses have gone up over the last two years.
- You've heard a rumor that a peer of yours (the know-it-all) got a salary increase recently. (This in and of itself is not a fact, but what is factual is that the rumor has had a detrimental effect on your morale.)
- The company has just gone through a difficult financial period, but things are beginning to look up.
- You were promised consistent raises by the man who hired you; however, he is no longer with the company.

You hate to have to ask for money; they should just give it to you when you deserve it!

Money has such an intense charge to it. Many people, it seems, are more comfortable talking about intimate sexual details than about how much money they make. Whether you are a good salary negotiator or not, being forced to remind your boss that it is time to talk about giving you a raise is unpleasant, plain and simple. But you have waited long enough; it's clear that Human Resources is not going to tap your boss on the shoulder and remind him, and you're becoming more frustrated every day. The burden is all on your shoulders.

But before jumping to conclusions about whether or not you should act now, continue on with the Circle.

Question 2: What's Negotiable?

Here's how you answered Question 2:

- You know times have been hard, so you're willing to accept a smaller increase.
- You don't even need a formal review; some informal feedback with a larger paycheck will do.
- You would be willing to forgo that great-sounding conference in Hawaii in exchange for a raise.
- You would be willing to accept a raise within the next three months—not require it immediately.
- The raise does not have to be retroactive to the date on which you were *supposed* to get one.

The truth is, in large part, you just want to feel appreciated. Feedback is scarce at your company (well, positive feedback, that is), so the additional money would be a definitive indication that you're doing a good job. And, yes, you realize you're making a pretty good salary now, but it's time to make more!

As you go through this question and the next, The Working Circle helps you to see what is really at the bottom of your discontent. And as you decide what is negotiable, you identify what might be bargaining chips in the ultimate discussion you will have with your boss (that is, if you decide to move in that direction).

In answering this question, you now realize that the timing and amount of your raise are almost less important to you than the raise itself and the recognition.

Move on to the next question, to help further clarify what you really want.

Question 3: What's Nonnegotiable?

These are the items you decided were nonnegotiable:

- The conversation between you and your boss has to take place *soon*.
- It is time now to receive additional money in some form— bonus or salary.
- You won't be put off any longer.
- It is not acceptable to be told that no one is getting raises right now.
- You will put your demand on the table and, if you keep getting put off, update your résumé and prepare to move on.
- If you are asked to wait a while longer, you will ask for the date to be put in writing.
- Your self-respect is at stake and you refuse to risk it much longer.

Oh my! Looking at your list of nonnegotiable items, it certainly sounds as if you are angry. You are! Fortunately, The

Working Circle will help you to address what you want to accomplish and, at the same time, prevent you from hurting yourself professionally.

By reviewing your answers to Questions 2 and 3, it looks as if you have a clear list of what is and what is not negotiable for you, so now you can move on to Question 4, where you have an opportunity to examine what knowledge you bring to this situation from all of your past experiences.

Question 4: What Have I Learned from Previous Experiences?

When you are angry or upset, it's hard to look back and figure out what you may have learned from the past. Your current boss is making you angry, that's all you're focused on now, and you feel more frustrated than ever. But by taking the time to revisit previous situations, to recall how you handled them, it will help you to better address the present problem.

Let's assume here, though, that this exact kind of thing has not happened to you before. However, you *can* remember when you were in college and you got a grade that you believed was unfair—an insult, even. You went to talk to the professor with your grade in hand and your emotions boiling over. Consequently, you blurted out your demands in anger. This just caused the professor to act more and more defensively, effectively shutting you down and denying any meaningful conversation. You walked away feeling worse than before, and the poor grade remained on your record.

What did you learn?

● When you approach someone with angry accusations, it puts the other person on the defensive, a self-defeating result.

- Making demands without letting the other person speak from his or her perspective usually ends up backfiring.

- Calm down before you go to someone about something he or she has done that upset you. This will help you assert what you need to and be able to think.

- You can still be angry, but pointing the finger or making accusations will not work.

Remembering this situation and the lessons you learned from it will enable you to better prepare for the conversation you plan to have with your boss.

Answering Question 4 is not about recalling how many irritating people you have dealt with in your life. It is about what you have learned from dealing with them. You are going into this situation with lots of experience. You want to be prepared, and you want to be successful in your negotiations. The fact that you believe you are right has nothing to do with it. Being right doesn't necessarily help you win; being smart does.

Don't forget: Your growing impatience can weaken you in the conflict. Move cautiously and with intelligence, building on past experience.

Question 5: How Do I Feel about the Situation?

Reminder: Question 5 asks how you feel since you started working the Circle. Answering this question ensures that you are prepared to move forward to designing a game plan.

- Do you feel that you have been thorough in answering the questions so far?

- Have you overlooked anything?

Let's see where you stand at this juncture:

- You resent the pompous guy at work who seems to have gotten more money, when you haven't even had a discussion about a raise with your boss.
- You really resent your boss for putting you in this spot.
- You are very uncomfortable about confronting your boss.
- You're concerned that a negative confrontation could result in a highly intolerable situation at work. (Might you even get fired?)
- You're envious of your friend who has a supportive manager.
- You are tired of busting your butt and not getting paid adequately.
- You feel ready to put together a plan to deal with this situation.

Knowing how you feel helps prevent you from being dominated by your emotions. For those of us who have a particularly hard time in situations like this, this is when you acknowledge that you might be afraid to do anything at all. The knowledge that this could cause you to become totally disheartened at work is tough to face. Tough, yes, but not insurmountable. After all, you are justified in asking to be remunerated adequately for your work.

For those of us who have trouble controlling our tempers, and can often say and do things that are rather blunt, this question gives us an opportunity to vent before going forward.

Let's move on to the plan.

Question 6: What's My Game Plan?

At last! You've reached the linear part of The Working Circle, where you take all of your previously determined perspectives and formulate a game plan. Taking into consideration what you answered to the first five questions, you now plan your behavior, your approach, and your words.

Since you can never anticipate another person's reactions, you can't plan what your antagonist will do. It never works to plan what words the other person will say or actions he or she will take, because once that person deviates from your preconceived notions, you can become stymied. Rather, you need to plan your approach and how to phrase things so that you can be a problem solver, not a problem maker. Therefore, in your planning, avoid the pitfall inherent to this tactic: "If I say . . . , then he'll say . . ." It never works!

You've determined that, based on what you listed as negotiable and nonnegotiable, you need to talk to your boss to resolve the issue of asking for a raise. If you don't do something soon, you know your resentment will continue to rise, which will only make matters worse.

You want to address your concerns, and using what you've learned from past experiences, minimize the chances that you will prompt a defensive reaction from your boss. You plan to:

- Approach your manager on a day and time of day when she is typically most approachable.
- *Not* use e-mail to voice your concerns; this is a person-to-person issue.
- Tell her that you will take no more than a half hour of her time, but that it must be without interruption, as the issue is very important to you. If she asks what it is you want to talk about, just say you will explain everything when you meet. ("I need to talk to you about something that is really important to me. How about this Thursday, at 11:00?") As you have gotten to know your boss better, you know which days and which times of day might work best.

- Prepare whatever data you need before the meeting—in this case, that would include:
  - Salary history
  - Earlier promises made to you in regard to raises
  - Any company policies that support your request
  - Successes and kudos you received over the past year
  - Possibly mention that you know others are receiving raises. This might backfire—sometimes managers don't want to appear that they are not as good as other managers. Use your judgment here!

With the beginning of your plan in place, now's a good time to go the Masculine-Feminine Continuum to give you a sense of the range of options for introducing the topic with your boss.

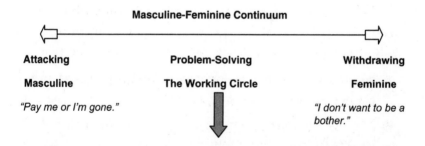

Masculine-Feminine Continuum

Attacking	Problem-Solving	Withdrawing
Masculine	**The Working Circle**	**Feminine**
"Pay me or I'm gone."		*"I don't want to be a bother."*

Note

For each of the eight challenges, the arrow will indicate a possible problem-solving approach for an opening statement. These suggestions reflect a balanced approach, in contrast to the extremes of either the masculine or feminine approach.

The Problem-Solving Approach When the time comes, start with something like, "Thanks for giving me this uninterrupted time. I have been quite concerned about the fact that my salary increase is overdue. I believe that I have been doing a good job: my last project got, as you know, terrific feedback from a number of senior managers. What I want to know, and be assured of, is exactly when can I expect to see an increase in my salary?"

Then, be prepared:

- To deal with resistance by being firm and insistent, but not confrontational.

- To illustrate how this issue is detracting from your ability to continue do a good job for your boss.

- To stand your ground without becoming defensive if your boss raises any issues about incidents in the past where you could have done better. Admit any mistakes you made, then continue to maintain your firm stance.

- To resist making demands, if things get tense. You *can* say, however, "I know what my value is, and it is extremely important for me to feel appreciated here." That statement lets her know implicitly that you are well aware you can work elsewhere; you don't have to state it directly, as that will come across as confrontational.

- To avoid answering directly if your boss asks if you are thinking of leaving. Instead, say something like, "I want to be here because I like the challenge. But that challenge just has to be met with appropriate compensation."

You can, if necessary, put a time frame on your request, by saying, for example, "I hope this can be resolved by the end of next month. It has been so frustrating for me; I would really like closure soon on this very important issue."

If your boss replies with a definitive no, thank her and move on. You now have decisions to make, but don't end the conversation by making any threats. You can, of course, demonstrate how disappointed, and even angry, you are, but keep it within the professional range that is acceptable in your company's culture.

If you hear a yes or "I'll look into it," schedule a follow-up meeting, to gain confirmation and closure. If this is the case, be sure to follow up on that date!

Once you have been told yes, you can explore the amount of the raise and/or bonus. That may be the start of another negotiation entirely. Regardless, if you have gotten this far, congratulations!

Don't forget, at this point, that in determining what was negotiable, you decided the amount of the raise was secondary to reaching an agreement that you deserved the increase/bonus. That said, if you do have a definite amount in mind, make sure that you state what it is, listen to the response from your boss, and be prepared to continue to negotiate based on what she says.

In this game plan, you have been assertive, professional, firm, and clear, both about what is bothering you and what you want. A word of caution is in order here, however: I learned a long time ago in these kinds of discussions that demonstrating all those wonderful qualities doesn't necessarily mean you will get what you want. Never forget, you always have a choice. You are a highly qualified professional, and you can, always, with patience, get what you are worth.

As you know by now, The Working Circle has eight questions, eight perspectives. At this stage in Challenge 1, you have two more questions to consider. They are important in rounding out your game plan, adding greater assurance that you will succeed and learn.

Word of Caution

When putting your game plan together, and when speaking to a boss or colleague, it's not appropriate to say such things as, "I don't want you to feel bad/angry/upset/and so on." That person is going to feel however he or she does feel, no matter what you say. But you can be assertive about how you are being treated, and how you feel. Trying to control how someone else feels is contradictory to constructive conflict resolution. I will talk about this more as we progress through the plan.

Let's move on to Question 7.

Question 7: What Transformations Will the Game Plan Bring?

Experiencing this kind of conflict is not easy. No matter what your Conflict Resolution Style, dealing with your manager about money is not what you wake up wanting to do. Learning from experience is what earns you some benefits from these situations (in addition to ultimately making more money!).

Question 7 asks you to look at the benefits you can get from your current game plan—and the situation itself. If you carry out the plan as outlined in the previous question, here are some of the benefits you might see:

- You might receive a salary increase or a bonus.
- You will have the opportunity to express yourself clearly to your boss, maintaining your professionalism while getting your points across.

- You demonstrate to both your boss and yourself that you cannot be easily put off or dismissed.
- You will learn how much (or little) your boss is willing to stand up for you.
- You might gain some clarity on how your performance is perceived, which will help you to make future decisions for yourself—professional development, career direction, and so on.
- You will have a better idea if this job, this company, is for you, or whether it's time to look for a new job.
- You maintain your self-respect.

Keep in mind, these are the benefits you gain whether or not you get the raise/bonus.

If there are other benefits you would like to gain from your game plan, return now to Question 6 and modify your answers. For example, if you now decide you would also like to speak to your manager's boss, there might be an opening in the discussion with your manager to request that all three of you meet—assuming such an action is acceptable in the corporate culture.

We now move on to Question 8, which allows you to project into the future: If this transformation occurs, what impact on my future will it have?

Question 8: Will These Changes Ultimately Be Positive?

Confronting this issue as outlined in your game plan enables you to become more assertive, direct yet nonconfrontational, and capable of asking for what you deserve. As you become more adept at this behavior, you will be respected more, viewed as a professional who is a no-nonsense kind of person, but one who is fair and able to listen even when upset.

Can this be anything but terrific for your future?

In my human resources and consulting roles, I have seen many, many people fired. (I really related to the main character in the movie *Up in the Air*! He traveled across the country firing people. In my last job, when we had to lay off 1,000 people, my nickname was, "Dr. Death.") I now believe that the predominant reason for people losing their jobs is that they tick off too many people. Look around you at work: I bet you can find at least one person who does a mediocre or unsatisfactory job, yet he or she remains on the payroll. Very often, these employees remain because they don't make waves or alienate others. (Of course, there are other reasons, but what I am describing happens a lot!) In fact, I have been there: I needed to learn how to be assertive without alienating, and that is why I now teach it.

When we turn away from issues of money, it leaves us feeling a lack of self-respect. Conversely, attacking others leaves us without the respect of others. We need both for long-term career success.

Chapter 5

Challenge 2

Deal with Your Partner or Allow Him/Her to Continue Causing Chaos?

There are some people who, by their very nature, cause problems. They may be sloppy, careless, inattentive, and/or unaware of their impact on others. What's clear is that when they leave a situation, things are usually worse than before their arrival.

Usually, these people mean well. I work under that assumption until proven otherwise. That is what this challenge is about: those people who instigate issues and make problems, and don't really mean to do so.

Note

For those people whom you suspect cause problems at your workplace intentionally, I recommend that you keep written records of your interactions with them, and go directly to your manager or to human resources to get support and backup for dealing with them.

Meet Les and Adam

To explain this challenge, I share with you the story of two partners—although it could just as well be about two coworkers or two managers on the same level of the org chart.

These two men are peers, who trust each other, became successful together, and then strayed off the path. Les and

Adam were partners in a small start-up technical company. They had been in business for three years, during which time revenues climbed at a steady pace. At the end of their third year, the company had 18 employees and an expected growth rate of 16 percent in the upcoming year. In order to accomplish this growth, they needed to institute more internal controls and processes and further define their respective roles so that they could maximize productivity and quality.

Les and Adam are good complements to one another: Les is a 38-year-old man with a wife and one child. He is a visionary, whose grand plans have helped the partners reach the level of success they have, to date. His favorite activity is to sit in his office, plan, review the financials, and then devise course corrections. He is extremely bright, and does not like chaos; he wants the future to unfold as planned. When you ask Les a question, you get a response that is to the point: no more, no less.

Adam is 36, married, with two kids. He met Les five years ago at a Wall Street firm where they both were working; they dreamed of becoming partners one day in their own company. Adam is the consummate salesman; he can sell anything, anywhere, to anyone. He is also one of those guys who really needs to be liked; you'll often find him walking around the offices with pride, joking and gossiping with the employees. He's equally known for his untidiness; his office is a total mess, and one learns quickly not to give Adam a document or file without keeping a copy for oneself.

As often happens in such partnerships, one is the "inside man" (Les) and the other is the "outside man" (Adam). When an entrepreneurial company grows quickly, shifting from informal to more formal processes is difficult, at best. Les and Adam's company needed to improve customer tracking and internal communications. Most important, the flow of work from client acquisition to customer service needed to be crystallized, or an increasing number of errors would be made.

Both Les and Adam followed individual routines when they came to the office: Les came in between 7:30 and 8:00 AM, made coffee, and retired to his office. Adam arrived somewhere between 8:30 and 9:00 AM. When Adam arrived, you could hear him saying hello to everyone as he made his way to his office. If an employee stopped him to talk, he took the time to do so. He loved to hear the office scuttlebutt and chit-chat—from intrigues that were occurring to clients who were pains in the neck to what last night's football score was.

If there were a conflict at the office, there was no question where one or the other of the disputants would go: to Adam's office. He would listen to the disputants complain about the other person involved, and sympathize with each of them, in turn. The result was that when each of the employees involved in the dispute left Adam's office, he or she was firmly convinced that Adam agreed with his or her take on the problem.

Gregarious as he was, Adam wasn't good at keeping secrets or maintaining confidences. He would share the details of the dispute with others in the office—although sometimes with the intent of using the conflict as an example of a situation others should avoid. One of the unintended consequences of his actions, however, was a growing mistrust employees felt for their colleagues. Besides, no one knew how they were expected to resolve conflict they had with others at work. On the contrary, the individual sessions that Adam held with employees inevitably caused only more mistrust, because he seemed to take sides, and he did not model helpful problem-solving behavior. Rather, he would try to address these issues by confronting one or another of the disputants, and give vague instructions such as, "You really should quit making Tom angry all the time." The person hearing this statement would usually become defensive, and more antagonistic toward Tom, because Tom had gone to Adam.

Adam also created chaos by cutting deals with new clients and then often failing to relate the particulars to Les. He was a superb salesman and so making deals was, for him, enticing—understandable, since he did it very well. Communicating the details to his partner was where he tripped up. Les would, for example, set up a new account, communicate to the appropriate employee, and subsequently find out that Adam had not given all the details he needed to know. Les was, of course, thrilled at how well Adam brought in business—it was, after all, the lifeblood of their company growth. He just wanted to be told about them, so he and the rest of the employees could carry out their part of the work adequately and appropriately.

All in all, Adam's dual roles—managing the staff and making sales—combined to form the core of the chaos. Because he was out of the office a great deal making sales calls, he was not always available for coaching, monitoring, and directing the staff. Furthermore, his great need to be liked by the staff interfered with his ability to deliver difficult messages, when necessary, to his employees.

Not surprisingly, over time, office discipline and morale broke down: some employees began coming in late for work, which then caused delays in the completion of projects, which led to resentment from those employees who did continue to come in on time and complete their work on schedule. The most telling effect of this lack of management discipline was seen in the increasing number of errors being made by certain members of the staff. Les noticed it first, as he was the one who closely monitored employees' results.

As mistrust and disgruntlement in the office grew, tension also built up between Adam and Les. Les would insist, "We have to talk." Adam would put him off, saying he had a sales call to make.

What impact did this tension between their bosses have on the employees? Being in fast-growth mode, confusion grew around who was supposed to do what. Additionally, as typically happens where organizational mistrust exists, information wasn't being communicated efficiently among the staff. Understandably, when two or more people are in conflict, they aren't as willing to share data and information with their colleagues as they should.

Clearly, it was time for Les and Adam to address their issues. Adam's style was to be confrontational; sometimes, he bordered on using an attack mode. Les, unfortunately, took a similar approach to conflict, so even those conversations between them that began quietly ended with both of them shouting at each other so loudly that everyone in the office heard them.

Enter The Working Circle

I was brought into the situation through word of mouth: Les knew another client of mine, who recommended that he contact me for help. After meeting both Les and Adam and hearing each of their perspectives, I introduced The Working Circle to them. I had to do minimal facilitation, as they both understood the process; all I had to do was gently guide them through it, as detailed here.

To ensure that the discussion between them would be productive, they agreed to the following:

- To meet offsite, on a Saturday morning, at Adam's house, where there would be no interruptions (Adam's wife would be out with the kids).

- To allow the other to finish speaking before starting to talk (they each had a habit of finishing each other's sentences).
- To each speak for himself and not make assumptions about the other.
- To ask questions, instead of interpreting motives of the other person.
- To avoid blaming and raising voices.

With Les and Adam's list of agreements in mind, let's now look at the Masculine-Feminine Continuum to examine traditional behaviors for this kind of situation.

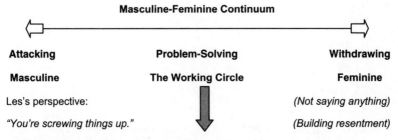

Masculine-Feminine Continuum

Attacking	Problem-Solving	Withdrawing
Masculine	**The Working Circle**	**Feminine**

Les's perspective: *(Not saying anything)*

"You're screwing things up."   *(Building resentment)*

"I want us to talk about how to make things work better. There are some ways that I think what we are doing is not playing to our respective strengths."

Adam's perspective:

"You don't do anything to help."   *(No longer listens to employees)*

"I know we need to talk and I'm ready to listen to you. Then I'll tell you what I need."

When I worked with Les and Adam, they agreed we would use The Working Circle when we sat down for the problem-solving session. I would guide them through the process (in the same way as I am for you here in the book), but the responsibility for the conversation between them was primarily theirs. I did, however, let them know that certain highly charged words and concepts would not be part of the conversation. These included:

Blaming

"You must"

"You should"

Raised Voices

"Other people say . . ."

"I feel that you . . ."

I encouraged them to instead make statements that began with:

"I need"

"I feel"

"I want"

Speaking for oneself engages the other person and is less likely to activate defensiveness.

Remember: This situation is about two partners. It could, however, relate to any two peers who work together and are experiencing conflict issues.

We'll now join Adam and Les on their journey through The Working Circle.

Question 1: What's the Situation?

Both men needed to remember that answers to this question must not include opinions. Fortunately, underneath their problems, they trusted each other and were highly motivated to make this situation work. That was in their favor, for sure.

Here are the points they agreed on in answering Question 1:

- They were both talented at what they did.
- The fast growth of their company necessitated documented processes that could be replicated.
- Not all employees were coming in on time, and some were making more errors.
- If the projected growth occurred, they would need to hire three to five more people, and they couldn't oversee 23 employees by themselves.
- Adam's paperwork was not in order.
- Les spent most of the day in his office; Adam spent most of his out in the field.
- Their friendship was suffering.
- They both wanted to succeed.
- Les was great with details.
- Adam was great at sales.

With this list in hand, they were ready to move on to the next question.

Question 2: What's Negotiable?

Here are the items Les and Adam agreed were negotiable:

- Who manages the staff.
- How processes get documented, so that they can be repeated.

- How sales information is transferred from Adam to Les.
- Start times for employees (i.e., can be staggered/flexible).
- Whether they can promote someone to a supervisory position.

It was clear to both Adam and Les when discussing what was negotiable that they agreed more than they disagreed on operating methods. They moved on to what was non-negotiable.

Question 3: What's Nonnegotiable?

Les and Adam's list of what was nonnegotiable was longer than the previous one. It included:

- The goals they set for the company.
- Adam's role as sales leader.
- Les's role as CFO.
- Processes that were formalized and institutionalized, so that they could be communicated to everyone consistently
- That the atmosphere at the company should not be so casual that it increased the chances of employee error.
- Conversely, the atmosphere at the company should not be so stiff that workers became uncooperative, mistrustful of one another, and so formal that everyone was tense.
- The employees had to be managed in such a way that they enjoyed working in the company; they had to be well trained, to ensure they performed in an optimum manner.
- The friendship between Les and Adam.
- Someone had to manage the staff efficiently and professionally, and it could be someone other than Les or Adam.

I noticed that as Adam and Les answered each question, they began to relax. They were not blaming each other, and they were each letting the other finish speaking before adding what he had to say. Their underlying trust and strong goal orientation resurfaced. They began to believe they would be able to come up with a game plan that worked for both of them and their employees.

At this time, however, as with most of my clients, I had to caution them to not jump into game plan design before they had answered all of the questions leading up to the game plan question. This is an important point: *Almost without exception,* both individuals and groups want to jump ahead to finding solutions before they have thoroughly explored their situation. If the partners had done that, they would have missed some important issues that needed to be uncovered—such as acknowledging that neither Adam nor Les had to be the manager of the staff. If they had overlooked that, they might not have been quite as creative as they ultimately were in devising their solutions.

In the case of Les and Adam, keeping them from jumping the gun was like holding two race horses from bolting—especially Adam, who could see the finish line before he saw the starting gate. Later, they grew to appreciate the process, but at this point in the discussion, it was visibly challenging for them! I mention this so that you are aware of this tendency when you walk the Circle.

Let's move on to Question 4.

Question 4: What Have I (They) Learned from Previous Experiences?

If Adam and Les had been working alone, they would not have considered this question. They discovered that looking at the situation from this perspective was enormously help-ful. They examined their previous successes and failures then applied the lessons they had learned from them. Without the Circle, they would have forged ahead, without stopping to review the past and what they had gained from their collective experiences. Here's what they came up with:

- Les remembered that when he was at the Wall Street firm, he performed more effectively when he interacted with other teams; doing so gave him a broader perspective and provided him with more data with which to make better decisions.

- Adam remembered a time when he intervened in an argument between his wife and his mother, hoping that he could help make peace between them. Not only did it *not* help, but they came to terms with each other without his help and ended up angry at him for interfering! Remembering this, he was reminded not to meddle.

- Both Les and Adam remembered one of the managers they had once worked for—a great guy—who scheduled regular team meetings to discuss how to improve things, and at which he welcomed everyone's input. What did the partners learn from working with this man? That the people who are in the trenches often have the most valuable input as to how to make things work more efficiently.

Before answering this question, both Adam and Les had forgotten some of these events, and connecting them now to the current situation brought new awareness for the partners. They were now ready to proceed to Question 5.

Question 5: How Do I (We) Feel about the Situation?

Here's where the partners stand at this point:

- Les has calmed down enough to believe that he and Adam can reach a viable solution.
- Adam has begun to see that some of his well-intended behavior was resulting in the opposite of what he wanted.
- Both Les and Adam are ready to create a game plan.

Question 6: What's My (Our) Game Plan?

The game plan ideas came fast and furious from both Les and Adam! Consequently, I had to remind them to let the other guy finish his thoughts. Still, their enthusiasm was contagious, as they came out with idea after idea—all the while referring to their responses to the previous five questions. The game plan they produced had a timeline, assigned responsibilities, and follow-up actions.

I admit, it was wonderful to be there and watch them engage successfully in conflict resolution with minimal facilitation from me at this point!

The main points of their game plan were as follows:

- Les would make an effort to get out of his office more often.
- Les would become the operations manager.
- Together, they would begin to structure the team managed by two supervisors, to lighten the load for both of them. Adam would hire a part-time assistant to help him with the administrative aspects of his job.
- They would meet formally once a week to discuss issues, problems, and ideas, and develop action plans.

- Adam would use his strong interpersonal skills to assist employees in resolving their issues together; he would no longer act as a go-between.
- They would develop a company policies and procedures manual, with a focus on consistency and maintaining a relaxed but productive and efficient work culture.
- Adam would hire another salesperson, and groom him/her for success.
- Les would counsel any employees who weren't performing adequately.
- At the end of the year, the partners would add an operations manager position, in order to take more of the day-to-day management tasks off their desks.
- They would hold a company meeting, at which they would inform the entire staff of their decisions and plans.

At first, it seemed to the partners as if they had a lot to do. When reviewing the game plan, however, they recognized that all of the actions in it positioned them for further growth. They were ready to spring into action, feeling greatly relieved. Of course, at this stage, I had to remind them that in order to solidify their game plan, they first needed to answer the final two questions.

Question 7: What Transformations Will the Game Plane Bring?

As the partners considered this question, something very interesting occurred. They began to see the wholeness of their enterprise—that their venture touched every part of their lives. As you read how they responded to this question, you will learn how they came to realize that their game plan would transform them, both professionally and personally.

Their responses:

- They would improve communication between them, building more trust and stability in the relationship and the business.
- Adam would learn to use his highly effective influence/sales skills in a more directed manner.
- Les would become more comfortable managing people and giving feedback.
- They would position the business for more growth, while maintaining the relaxed atmosphere Adam and Les preferred.
- They would both learn to delegate more—a critical skill for successful entrepreneurs.
- They would ultimately feel more relaxed, at home and in social situations with each other, as there would be no lingering tensions between them.

By working the Circle, Les and Adam moved through a conflicted situation into clarity, as well as personal and professional enhancements! Unquestionably, they were ready for Question 8.

Question 8: Will These Changes Ultimately Be Positive?

As happens so often, answering this question served as an affirmation especially of their game plan, but also the entire process for Les and Adam.

But before we leave these two, I want to add an important footnote in regard to this particular situation. All of us can find it extremely difficult to confront a situation that involves a peer, professional friend, or partner. We may jump to conclusions about how the other person will react, and our concern over our ability to deal with conflict may be magnified when peers are involved, because we value these relationships highly and don't want to disrupt them.

In fact, dealing with this kind of conflict is especially important because it touches on both our professional and personal lives. "I thought I could trust you" is a phrase I have heard often in this situation—even between husband-and-wife business partners. These multilayered relationships make communication more complex and more charged, and so more important to resolve.

Having a process that eases these difficult conversations is so very helpful. Les and Adam used the language of The Working Circle (e.g., "Okay, let's get to a game plan, partner!") to resolve their conflicts. As a result, there was more lightness between them, and even when there was conflict, they were confident they could work things out. More, their collaborative conflict resolution behavior was contagious: their employees saw that the bosses could do it, and soon everyone became more cooperative.

As I write this book, Les and Adam have completed another year with tremendous success, beating their revenue projections. They continue to use The Working Circle as a template for decision making and resolving conflict.

Bravo to the brave-hearted who are willing to initiate a challenging conversation!

Chapter 6

Challenge 3

Speak Up about What's Happening or Remain Silent?

What happens when you have to defend your organization to an outsider, all the while knowing that what your company did was not right?

How difficult is it to defend the actions of your boss to a subordinate when you disagree with the boss?

How do you handle a meeting where you know one of the participant's lies may cause great damage?

These are situations that can keep us up at night. This isn't a book about ethics; however, ethics and conflict often form a symbiotic relationship, one feeding upon the other. We face a very real dilemma when we witness something that undermines the success of the organization in the long term. The dilemma becomes even more poignant when what we observe has the potential to undermine our personal success.

This challenge isn't about those situations where laws or regulatory practices are broken. In those cases, each of us has a moral and legal obligation to take action. Still each of us has personal decisions to make and no one can guide us but our conscience. It's easy to say, "Take action!" It's the taking action that's hard. In those very difficult circumstances, I suggest you move ahead carefully, get sage and/or legal advice, and be as brave as you can be.

Here, I want to focus on those more frequent occasions where your actions might be at odds with your conscience. No laws or regulations are being broken, but the actions of another person or the organization are, you believe, unethical.

An example: A number of years ago, I was at a regional review meeting at a company I worked for, watching a dog and pony show, where key leaders of the region were reporting on business results to the national leader of the business. Also present was the CFO—my peer, the regional VP, and his two top directors. It was obvious the regional VP wanted to put everything in the best light possible. One of the four account executives stood and discussed his major accounts. One of the accounts, he boasted, had been obtained by lying to the customer. He stated this quite plainly, with a broad smile on his face. I couldn't help but notice, as he was saying this, the company values prominently displayed on the wall, in a beautiful framed plaque. After this account executive finished his spiel, he left the room. The four of us—the regional VP, my boss, the CFO, and I—were seated at the conference table.

"Is this a usual practice?" I asked the group, referring to the account exec lying to a prospect. No one answered. I pushed a little harder: "Am I the only one who is bothered by this?" To my amazement, still no one answered. Tom, the regional VP, began instead to speak on a new topic, and the meeting went on without any acknowledgment of my queries.

Unfortunately, this kind of practice was rather common at this company. I believe it was part of the reason the company did so poorly: no one trusted anyone else; the culture was one of "every man for himself." Such behavior undermines the collective focus on company goals.

Why are there so many failing organizations in U.S. business? One of the most cogent reasons is greed. Too many people share the outlook that: "Everybody cuts their own deals. I want my piece of the action, and I want as much as I can get, as quickly as I can get it. The company doesn't care about me, so why should I care about it?"

But that's building a house of cards, and, ultimately, if the majority continues to act in that manner, the house of cards will tumble down. Our entire economy almost fell all the way to the ground not so long ago, and this was after so many supposedly in the know believed there could be no down cycle.

If, instead, we deal professionally and appropriately with situations that raise ethical questions, we can support ourselves, maintain our values, and help the organizations we work for to succeed. And if we work for a firm where unethical practices are the norm, we need to ask ourselves why we are working there.

Assume you witness an activity that is clearly not kosher. This knowledge makes you nervous, understandably! It feels as if you are holding a ticking bomb. Along with recognizing that this might be unethical and/or against company's values, you also worry about yourself, even if you didn't participate in what you saw. You think, "If I say something, I could anger someone or, worse, lose my job." You might even think, "Does anyone want to hear what I have to say?"

I believe that you can say something, if you plan and act wisely. You might even come to be regarded as a hero, but that shouldn't be your motivation, and certainly isn't my motivation in telling this story. My motivation is *always* that the organization succeeds and thrives and that its employees are valued. In the story relating to this challenge, I demonstrate how The Working Circle can help you deal with just such a situation, without shooting yourself in the foot.

Meet Aimee

Aimee was a customer service trainer for a medium-sized electronic parts firm. She traveled to offices across the country, providing training for sales and service representatives. She had been in her job for a year and a half. Her supervisor was a no-nonsense kind of guy, who pushed hard to get the training completed and satisfy each local manager. Aimee liked him well enough, though there wasn't much socializing in the department, because everyone (three trainers) was on the road most of the time.

While Aimee was conducting a class at the Atlanta office, she was told something that upset her. The reps were bragging that their region had led the division for 12 months straight—they certainly seemed proud. Then, during a break in the class, one of the participants was talking to Aimee, and alluded to the fact that the reps had been instructed by their manager to double-count certain electronic components so that the numbers would add up to more than they actually were. Aimee listened, and then asked the rep how he felt about that.

"Not good; but what can you do? If you speak up, you will lose your job," was his response. "Besides, we get a good bonus for our production, and I don't want to lose that, either."

Aimee was disturbed by this conversation. She knew of other representatives in other regions who were working just as hard, but could not match the results of this region. Now she knew why: this region's manager was fudging the results.

During the next part of the class, she picked up other clues that led her to believe that what she had been told was true.

She called her manager in New York. (This was definitely not content for an e-mail!) She told him what she had discovered, and asked what he thought should happen.

"If management doesn't catch it, it's none of our business," Aimee's boss told her. That didn't satisfy Aimee. She had friends in other regions who weren't getting the bonuses they deserved because of the practices in the Atlanta office, dictated by its manager, who also seemed to be intimidating his staff, and made them complicit with this double-counting.

Aimee remembered other company meetings she had attended where the leadership had made a point of the high ethical standards at the firm. The last such speech, given by the COO, relayed the message that it was incumbent upon each and every employee to "do the right thing."

What to do? Aimee's manager's boss, the VP of human resources, was a rather stiff and unapproachable individual, and Aimee was a bit intimidated by her. She wondered where this VP would stand on an issue like this.

She also considered the national VP of sales, who was a gregarious, friendly man. Aimee had met him, but had not had much contact with him in the past. Still, she thought, if anyone would be concerned about this issue, it should be him!

Enter The Working Circle

Aimee decided to go to The Working Circle to determine what she would, or would not, do.

Question 1: What's the Situation?

Before she "walked" around the Circle, Aimee reviewed the numbers for the six regions in the country. The results of the Atlanta region had far surpassed the other five regions for more than a year, and consequently the sales team there had received kudos from senior management, plus bonuses galore.

There were a lot of emotions surrounding this situation for Aimee. She reminded herself to answer Question 1 by acting as if she were a camera, taking snapshots of the circumstances.

The aspects of the situation she captured were:

- It was highly probable that the Atlanta region was double-counting some results to appear to lead the country in sales.
- The participant in Aimee's class who divulged the information to her was too frightened to do anything about the situation himself.
- Aimee's manager would not pass the information up the food chain.
- It was entirely up to her whether to address this situation.
- Aimee's friends in other regions were not getting remunerated as they deserved because of the tactics of the Atlanta office.
- Aimee felt she had a moral and ethical responsibility to do something, but was also concerned that if she did, it might hurt her career at the company.
- If she did nothing, there would be no damage to her career; her boss had assured her of that.
- Aimee was angry at the Atlanta regional manager for (probably) being an unethical leader.

As she answered this question, Aimee felt like she was between a rock and a hard place. Do nothing? Do something? She decided to calm her concerns and continue on with the Circle.

Question 2: What's Negotiable?

Aimee wrote down the following items as being negotiable in solving the conflict she faced:

- Whether she did something about the situation was totally negotiable—the ball was in her court.
- If she decided to take action, whom she approached was negotiable.
- If she decided to do something, when she did it was negotiable.
- Aimee knew very well that values in a corporation could be negotiable, depending on who the leader was and which polices were being reinforced in the company. To date with this company, she had seen most people walking their talk.

It wasn't a long list, as it seemed to Aimee that very few aspects were negotiable for her. This made her feel like she was tiptoeing through a minefield.

Question 3: What's Nonnegotiable?

Aimee's list of nonnegotiable items was much longer.

- Number one, Aimee's values weren't negotiable. She had been raised by wonderful parents, who taught her it was better to lose than to win by cheating.
- Expecting her boss to address the situation was definitely out of the picture.
- It was becoming more and more clear to Aimee that if she did nothing, she would be disappointed in herself.
- The company's values were portrayed as nonnegotiable from, "Do the right thing!" to, "We are honest and ethical in everything we do." The plaque was on the wall for all to see.
- Aimee's loyalty to her friends was nonnegotiable: she wanted to help them get what they were working so hard for, and deserved.

⊛ She didn't in any way want to implicate her manager. No one had to know that she had spoken to him at the outset.

⊛ Her loyalty to the company was nonnegotiable, as well—as long as she was being treated fairly and equitably. In the year and a half she had been an employee, this had been the case, so her loyalty was intact.

Question 4: What Have I Learned from Previous Experiences?

Aimee was 33 years old. She had been raised in a Midwestern town where there were fewer students in her high school than there were in her apartment building in New York City. She had grown up believing that with hard work, one could succeed. Within a week after arriving in New York to start work at her first corporate job, she had had her purse stolen on Broadway. Over the 11 years she had lived in the city, she had become less trusting and more skeptical.

In particularly difficult and/or sticky circumstances, this question asks us to search our life experiences for lessons we have learned and how they might be applied to the current situation. At times, what comes to our mind may seem remote and disconnected to the current dilemma, but I have learned that if I think of it, I'll find it has meaning and relevance. The lesson we learned is the key.

Two incidents came to Aimee's mind as she considered this question.

The first occurred when she was 10 years old. One of the students in her fifth grade class had been stealing from the other children. By accident, Aimee discovered who it was and told the teacher, quietly and in confidence. The culprit was caught and punished, and Aimee was rewarded by her teacher, her best friend, and her parents.

The second incident took place at a conference Aimee had attended three years earlier. Lily Ledbetter, who had filed a gender discrimination suit against Goodyear, spoke at the conference. In describing her travails, she impressed Aimee deeply. How someone could risk so much?

Recalling these incidents in response to Question 4 about learning from experience reinforced Aimee's anger at the Atlanta regional manager. It also clarified for her that she would likely have to do something. But what? She still couldn't answer that, as she moved on to Question 5.

Question 5: How Do I Feel about the Situation?

Here's how Aimee answered this question:

- She wished that she had not found out about the probable unethical behavior.
- She was worried what the repercussions might be to her for taking action.
- She was, nevertheless, bound to do something, for speaking out, addressing the situation, aligned with her values and the stated values of the corporation.

Answering Question 5 cemented her decision: she would make a game plan, and it would involve her speaking out about what might be a very serious unethical practice taking place at the Atlanta office.

Question 6: What's My Game Plan?

Aimee knew the difference between being brave and being foolhardy, and kept this in the front of her mind as she considered her game plan. Together with two close friends, sitting in her living room one evening, she began to lay out the plan. They were very helpful and very supportive; they also raised issues that she had overlooked, which was extremely beneficial.

The plan they developed contained these actions:

- Contact George, the VP of sales, and ask for an appointment, at which time Aimee would to fill him in on information that might be helpful to the sales force.
- She would mention the meeting in her weekly status report to her boss *after* she met with George, thereby in no way implicating him—that he had chosen not to address the situation.
- At the meeting with George, the sales VP, she would assert that she wanted the discussion to be kept in confidence.
- She would tell George what she had discovered in Atlanta, but not divulge the name of the individual who told her.
- She would be clear that she had no hard evidence, but that she thought it viable enough to at least warrant an investigation by George.
- Aimee would ask George to keep her out of the situation— that is, she wished to remain anonymous.
- She decided she would not tell anyone else at work what she was intending to do.

The next morning, Aimee planned to call the sales VP's office and get on his calendar. She hoped she would not have to wait too long until they could meet.

Question 7: What Transformations Will the Game Plan Bring?

All Aimee could really focus on at this point was what personal transformation might result from her decision to move ahead in confronting the situation. Anything beyond that was out of her control.

This is important to keep in mind when we respond to this question: The only person we can control is ourselves. In dealing with others, we can wonder about the potential transformation our actions might bring to us; we cannot expect others will change. In Aimee's situation, she could *hope* that practices in the Atlanta regional office would change (if the allegations were proven to be true), but that wasn't her response to this question.

Question 7 asks us to look at how *we* will change, or be changed, by our decision—perhaps in our confidence, how we act toward others, or how we feel about and perceive ourselves.

In pondering this question, then, here's what Aimee came up with:

- In a competitive world, which seemed to produce mistrust of others, she would show herself to be an ethical, trustworthy person.
- She believed she would feel proud and confident in a way she hadn't felt in quite a while.
- She hoped she might help right a wrong at the company, even as she recognized that was unlikely to happen.

Her game plan seemed to reaffirm the Aimee she remembered from fifth grade: brave and willing to do what was right for the greater benefit of all. Now, she thought, she was beginning to sound like a girl scout, so she was quick to remind herself that this was business, not elementary school—and who knew what else might happen?

Question 8: Will These Changes Ultimately Be Positive?

Aimee's answer to this question was split: On the one hand, her game plan would ultimately have a positive effect on her perception of herself as an honest professional, loyal friend, and a woman who tries to do the right thing. On the other hand, she had no idea what moving forward might do to her career; would she become a pariah, an outcast, and eventually have to leave the company? She didn't think so, but she wasn't 100 percent sure.

Let's examine the Masculine-Feminine Continuum to see the contrast in approaches for Aimee with George, the sales VP.

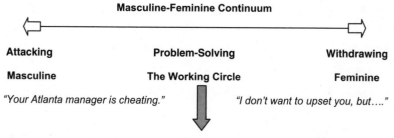

Masculine-Feminine Continuum

Attacking	Problem-Solving	Withdrawing
Masculine	The Working Circle	Feminine

"Your Atlanta manager is cheating."   *"I don't want to upset you, but...."*

"I need to talk to you about something that is really important. Let me tell you what I heard, and then I'm open to your comments, questions, and concerns."

Here's how this challenge played out:

When Aimee got in to see George, and after some small talk, she told him she needed to speak to him in confidence, as per her game plan. After he agreed, she said to him: "I heard some disturbing information when I was in Atlanta. I am not sure it is true, but I decided to let you know, just in case it is. I know you will do what you think is best and I request that I remain anonymous. I will not speak of this to anyone else. I heard that the Atlanta regional manager is double-counting sales results so that his region will lead the country."

Their conversation continued for another 15 minutes, after which Aimee left his office, feeling both very nervous and very relieved. Three months later, the Atlanta regional manager was transferred to another position in the company. Three months after that, he left the company. George never said anything to Aimee again, but he did give her a handshake at the next national sales meeting, and a very big smile. Aimee was proud of herself and the company she worked for.

Chapter 7

Challenge 4
Mediate or Take a Side?

It isn't comfortable watching other people argue in front of you. Maybe you want one person to prevail, maybe not. You certainly don't want to get in the middle: *the one in the middle gets the bullet hole!* Earlier in my life, I tried to get in the middle, and was amazed that both sides ended up angry at me! After a number of unexpected bruises, I stopped going there.

Mediating is not putting yourself in the middle; it is facilitating discussion and problem solving. Mediators hold a position of neutrality—more accurately, they *approximate* neutrality, since it is almost impossible to be totally neutral. The best we can expect to do, as mediators, is keep our biases at bay and interfere as little as possible in the reconciliation process.

When two people at work are at war—or worse, when there are warring factions—the organization suffers, as do individuals. Information doesn't flow the way it should, and, as we all know, information is key to any organization's success. I believe that another reason, beyond greed that so many organizations go astray is due to all of the internal wars that go on. Often at such companies, the leaders don't try to stop the conflict, much less teach the combatants to problem solve; they either turn a blind eye or support one side over the other. In this way, they deliver a message to the troops that it's acceptable to argue, but just make sure you are on the winning side. Or, put another way, disagreements are okay, as long as you are right. And we know that being right usually can be determined only in hindsight.

Working around two people (or two teams) that are at war can be awkward, personally as well as professionally. The discomfort grows more extreme when the conflict hampers your ability to do your job. Also, as conflict heats up, either side might look to you to become its ally.

Remaining neutral is definitely a skill you can develop. People who are viewed as neutral often have a perceived strength, as they can communicate with either side of the conflict with relative ease. Obviously, once you take a side, you risk alienating the opposition.

Taking a side on an issue that you feel strongly about one way or the other is an experience we have all had. You agree with one side and so align yourself with others who feel the same way. What becomes critical is *how* you and your allies participate in the disagreement. Acting as a person with integrity and values will take you a long way, especially if your side does not prevail. Keep in mind, you will have to work with these adversaries again, once the issue has been resolved. If your side is victorious, those you disagreed with will be more likely to be cooperative in the future if you competed with integrity and with respect for all concerned. This is not naïve, I assure you. Over the long term, it is those professionals who have integrity *and* an intense drive that others respect.

I began working with one company when it was two years into a merger. When employees referred to "we," they meant the company they *used* to work for, not the merged entity. Alliances were based on which company you came from, thereby inhibiting a collaborative incorporation of the two firms, which had been successful as individual entities. When I asked an employee how a process was carried out, for example, I was told, "This is the way we did it, and it is much better than the way they do it."

Destructive Conflict versus Healthy Competition

We are discussing destructive conflict in this challenge, which is very different from healthy competition between teams (or people). Healthy competition is good for the organization: it motivates excellence. When the conflict becomes the focus, however, and provokes unethical behavior, the organization suffers. In addition, once it becomes more important for the combatants to "win" than to accomplish organizational goals, they are engaged in destructive conflict, and the company is the ultimate loser.

On the upside, management did institute training classes and distributed newsletters in an effort to promote a more cooperative working environment, in an attempt to make the merger successful. On the downside, performance reviews and compensation practices did not match up; they did not reward collaboration, but individual effort. As a result, astute employees and managers who knew the value of collaboration built alliances with the other side. I observed that the ongoing conflict slowed down the progress of the merger, and cost the combined company a great deal in lost productivity. Leadership, with all good intentions, took the stance of a parent: "Now play well, all of you!"

I had another experience relating to this challenge, one in which I got caught in the crossfire. When I worked in human resources, my team was charged with supporting multiple business units. At one company, I worked for two senior managers who hated each other—I do mean *hate*! Clearly, I had to remain neutral, as I reported to both of them. One of the men complained about the other; the second man never trusted me because he thought I might pass along confidential information to his foe. I was caught in the middle, and so was my staff. Still, I was careful *never* to speak critically of either man to *anyone*.

The conflict between these two managers prevented, among other things, the amicable transfer of employees from one unit to the other, successful cross-selling and adequate implementation of companywide initiatives. After a number of months in the job, I offered to sit down with them both, in an effort to get them to address some of the business (not personality!) issues coming between them.

Business was being negatively affected for both of them in part due to their disagreements, so they agreed. We met on neutral territory, and covered basic business and HR issues. We came up with a plan, and my team and I ensured impartial support for its success. Subsequently, although there was a lot of slipping and sliding (senior management tacitly encouraged the conflict), things did improve. They improved because each man was highly motivated to succeed, and my mediation highlighted the need for them to collaborate on some issues, and this gave both of them a better chance to meet their objectives.

Throughout this book, I hope you have noticed that courage is one of the hallmarks of the stories I share with you. I feel strongly about being courageous—prudently courageous. I have known many people who have exhibited great courage in dealing effectively with conflict at work. This challenge, "Mediate or take a side?" has an underlying question: "What do you have the courage to do when other people around you are in conflict?" Taking action does not necessarily imply having courage. Wisdom is a far stronger indicator of courage, and that means knowing when to act and when not to.

Recognizing there is nothing you can do to alleviate a situation takes wisdom *and* courage. Taking sides out of expediency demonstrates pragmatism, which is often necessary to keep one's job—and one's sanity. Deciding to mediate likewise takes courage, and doing it effectively takes wisdom. We all need to maintain our self-respect and integrity in the face of conflict.

Enough said on these points. On with the story relating to this tricky challenge.

Meet Brian

Brian was a sales representative for an insurance broker. He had been selling property and casualty insurance for four years, and enjoyed the work. Recently, the brokerage had not been doing well, and the agency had to let a number of salespeople go. After the layoffs, Brian was required to sell property/casualty *and* health insurance. That meant he now had two managers, one for each product line. Bill (property and casualty) had been Brian's manager for a year; Erin (health) was his new boss. They were very competitive with each other.

The prospects Brian needed to call on were different for each product line. Leadership in the company assumed (as leadership often does) that the new arrangements would work out just fine; they expected everyone to understand these were trying times.

Under stress, people tend to become either heroes or villains. Stress brings out the best or the worst in us. In this case, it did not bring out the best in Bill and Erin, much to Brian's chagrin.

When Bill gave Brian his sales goals after the new arrange-ment went into effect, he made it clear that he resented that Brian would now be working only 50 percent of the time for him. He had modified the goals slightly to reflect that. Brian was assured that he could accomplish these goals, as they were more modest than they had been in the past. As already noted, Bill had been Brian's manager for the last year, and they got along well. Bill was a regular kind of guy; he worked hard, had a family, coached Little League, and basically worked a nine-to-five day, most days. Bill was not a star at the firm, but he was a steady producer. In the past, Brian would have preferred that Bill be more aggressive with sales, but Bill consistently took the middle-of-the-road approach, preferring safety to spectac-ular results. His sales were always good.

Erin, in contrast to Bill, had big plans for herself. She did not respect Bill; he was milquetoast to her. She wanted to rise up in management, and with Brian now reporting to her, she believed she could increase her numbers, on the back of his efforts. Erin was willing to do what it took to increase sales, and when she sat down with Brian, she told him so.

"Go out there and kick butt! Now is the time to sell group insurance," she said, taking into account what had been happening in Washington in regard to health care. She believed that now was the time to sell the affordable products the agency offered.

Erin also told Brian that if he exceeded the goals set for him, she would ensure that he would be promoted to a management position within a year. That promotion would give Brian more responsibility, as well as more money, which he certainly needed, with a baby on the way. But then she added a comment that changed the tenor of the conversation.

"Don't tell Bill that I spoke to you about the possible promotion," Erin confided to Brian. "He's not going anywhere, and he's lucky he wasn't included in the layoffs." At this point, Brian became uncomfortable with the conversation. He liked Bill and knew how much he needed his job. Moreover, the office gossip about Erin was that though the owners of the agency liked her, she was regarded as a "dragon lady"; she took no prisoners. Brian began to wonder how this split in his responsibilities was going to work out.

Over the next three months, the tension mounted. Erin and Bill gave Brian conflicting directions, and they began to criticize each other in front of Brian, which caused him even greater discomfort. Adding to Brian's stress level was that both Bill and Erin wanted more and more of his time and effort. He started to feel as if he were being stretched in two directions, and that he could easily fail both managers as their demands and expectations of him grew.

As the conflict intensified, both Bill and Erin would ask Brian questions about the other. Each also leaned on Brian to not move as quickly for the other. If, for example, Brian had a good week with one product line, the opposing manager would chide him for not working hard enough for him or her. The environment grew steadily more tense, at the same time the agency's results were not improving significantly, raising fears of more layoffs.

Brian now believed that the managers wanted more of him not just to improve the results of their divisions, but to outdo the other. He also realized that to meet each manager's expectations, he would probably have to work a 70-hour week! He was becoming more and more concerned about his future; how could he possibly succeed in such a contentious environment? If he fell short, would Erin blame him and make him the fall guy? Was Bill strong enough to keep his job with the agency? How would that affect Brian's prospects?

Brian tried to explain to Bill and Erin, in separate conversations, that their conflict was making it harder for him to succeed, for them and for himself. Bill was compassionate, but insisted that property and casualty was where Brian needed to direct his focus. For her part, Erin continued to remind Brian that if he wanted to succeed, he would have to ride on her coattails.

Brian had to figure out what he could do—if anything. He had approached Tom, the senior manager, one day, *very casually*, and hinted at the conflict between his two managers. Tom merely laughed and said, "May the best man, or woman, win!" He was not going to get any help there, thought Brian. Tom was flaming the fires of the conflict to increase results; everybody knew he loved a good fight.

The questions before Brian were: "Should I take sides? Should I do nothing? Should I attempt to mediate?"

Enter The Working Circle

Brian and I went to The Working Circle.

Question 1: What's the Situation?

Here's how Brian answered Question 1:

- He wanted to succeed, and one day move into management.
- Brian liked Bill, but was wary of Erin.
- Brian did not want to get in between Bill and Erin's conflict.
- Senior management was encouraging the conflict between Bill and Erin, hoping it would increase revenue.
- The conflict and tension was growing worse between Bill and Erin, and for Brian, too.

- If things continued the way they were going, Brian's ability to succeed would be hampered, as each manager wanted more and more of him.
- Brian liked Bill better than Erin, but Erin might be more successful at the agency in the long term.
- This was a messy situation at best, and at worst could cost him his job.
- He wasn't enjoying his job anymore.
- This was not the best time to look for another job, although that might become a possibility in the future (when the economy improved and after the baby was born).
- Brian felt stuck. He was working very hard, yet wasn't producing the results he would have liked in either product line.
- Brian believed he could work for either Erin or Bill, but working for both of them was becoming intolerable.

Question 2: What's Negotiable?

Brian listed these items as being negotiable in resolving the conflict he was facing:

- Brian was willing to sell either property and casualty or health insurance—he liked both.
- He had a good relationship with Bill—a general level of trust existed between the two men—and so he felt he had some leeway in what he said to him.
- An offsite meeting, scheduled for a month out, might offer a good opportunity for Brian to sit down with both his managers, if he decided to go forward.

● Brian didn't necessarily see himself working at this agency long term; certainly, if things didn't improve, he was open to going elsewhere when it became feasible for him.

As Brian listed his negotiable items, he started to feel less trapped. Whether he took action or not, he knew that, eventually, the economy would improve, his baby would be born, and he could go elsewhere, if need be. With this more positive outlook, he continued around the Circle.

Question 3: What's Nonnegotiable?

Most people working the Circle have an easier time figuring out what is nonnegotiable than what is negotiable. Brian was no exception:

● He was unwilling to compromise his values for either Bill or Erin.

● Although Brian liked Bill more than he did Erin, he would not take sides. That was far too dangerous in this uncertain environment.

● Brian wanted to remain neutral; he preferred that position and felt it to be a more professional stance to take.

At this point, the question regarding the situation changed for Brian. He had begun by asking: "Should I take sides? Should I do nothing? Should I attempt to mediate?" It was clear now to him that he would not, and should not, take sides. That was not an option, for he could not be sure which way things would wind up at the agency.

Brian continued answering what was nonnegotiable for him.

- In no way did he want to jeopardize his career in insurance.
- He did not intend to leave the agency until after his baby was born. Changing benefit plans midway in his wife's pregnancy was not advisable.
- He was determined to succeed; failure was not an option.

Reviewing his responses to this question, Brian became bolder still. Somehow, knowing how and where he would put his foot down made him feel more in charge, and less trapped in the conflict between Bill and Erin. He also became clearer that his preference for one manager over the other really had nothing to do with addressing the situation; he was well aware that alliances shifted all too easily in an uncertain environment.

Question 4: What Have I Learned from Previous Experiences?

As soon as Brian asked himself this question, a memory from his childhood popped into his mind. He was the middle child in his family, and his older sister and younger brother were always fighting. When they were kids, Brian's siblings used him as bait to incite one another. Consequently, Brian often felt angry and taken advantage of—caught in the middle. He realized how similar the current situation was.

What had Brian learned from his childhood experience? His parents, like senior management, were of very little help to him. They were not home a lot; both worked to provide for the family. Brian complained to his siblings, but they were so embroiled in their own conflict that they weren't really aware of the effect it was having on their brother. Brian felt helpless. His solution was to avoid his siblings as much as he could, but this, too, left him feeling angry, helpless, and lonely.

The lesson Brian learned was that being helpless left him feeling empty, and caused him to withdraw. As an adult, this was definitely *not* what he wanted to carry over into his professional life.

Learning from Life

I touched on this earlier, but it is worth repeating here in the context of this challenge. That is, when looking into the past to see what we have learned from our experiences, childhood events such as Brian recalled might at first seem trivial to us. But keep in mind that we all learn very early in our lives how to cope with things. Our knowledge about how to deal with conflict also begins very early. So whether we have 30 years of work experience or 3, our life experiences can provide a wealth of information in how to cope with conflict. My point is, if a childhood or young adult experience comes to mind when you ask yourself Question 4, I recommend you examine it carefully and reflect upon what it might mean. I believe strongly that if it came to your mind, you will find it has applicability to your current situation.

Answering Question 4 raises another important point, which many of my clients prefer to run through or avoid totally, relating to hindsight. We often learn from the consequences of our past decisions, whether or not they worked the way we wanted. (Note that I deliberately avoid using the word "right." My point here is about where the consequences of our decisions have taken us, not whether we were "right" or "wrong." If we could minimize such binary-type thinking, we all would become better conflict resolvers.)

Hindsight gives us insight, knowledge, as well as the ability to correct our courses. Asking "What did I learn from previous experiences?" opens us up to learning and closes the door to blaming. Blaming does not encourage learning; rather, it encourages avoidance and, for some, dishonesty. When was the last time you attended a meeting at work and the past was used as a foundation for learning and discussion?

Back to Brian   Before he moved on to the next question, Brian remembered another circumstance that he thought might shed light on his current situation. When he was working at his first job out of college, two peers who were in conflict asked him to step in and mediate between them. They trusted Brian, and preferred talking to him over going to management. Although Brian felt he had no skills as a mediator, he agreed to try to help. Over a few beers, and with Brian's help, the two peers came to a resolution. They were very grateful to Brian, and thanked him over and over. From Brian's point of view at the time, all he did was ask questions and let them talk.

Now, remembering this event, Brian thought that he might be able to facilitate a conversation between Bill and Erin—if it could take place in a relaxed setting, such as the upcoming retreat the company was planning. And, as he responded to each question in The Working Circle, he was growing bolder about taking action.

Looking into past experiences was helping Brian expand his perspective on the present situation. His confidence was growing that this very sticky situation might be resolved, and not necessitate his looking for a new job.

That's another valuable aspect of The Working Circle: it offers hope for finding solutions to difficult problems. I've seen client after client begin with little hope they could arrive at a satisfactory or peaceful resolution to their problem. Then, as they work through the Circle, I see their hope begin to resurface. In my experience over 14-plus years using the Circle, I've discovered that for most situations, (excluding dangerous situations or those involving rigid or disturbed individuals), this collaborative problem-solving approach works. The process, along with the introduction of a collaborative, non-accusatory language, makes resolution of even the most conflicted situation possible. Have faith!

At first, Brian felt a little silly relating past experiences to the present. But he came to understand that those memories were providing confirmation of his abilities. With renewed confidence, he moved on to the next question.

Question 5: How Do I Feel about the Situation?

When Brian arrived at this question, he stopped to ponder before beginning to answer it. People didn't ask "feeling" questions at work, and, truth be told, he generally preferred not to reveal how he felt. So he found himself resisting answering this question.

To help him through this impasse, I asked him a few peripheral questions.

"How do you feel now versus how you felt when you started with The Working Circle?"

"More confident and a little more relaxed", he responded. "At the same time, I am on edge about determining what I am going to do."

His response was completely understandable. One can feel better about something while still being anxious about what to do.

To prompt him once more, I asked, "If you review your answers to the first four questions, how do you feel about what you have said so far?"

Brian took a moment to go through his notes (which he had been taking as we went along, an activity I highly recommend). As a result, he went back to his nonnegotiable list and added another item. (For convenience, I included the item in the list of responses to Question 3.)

One of the purposes of this question is to allow us to take a moment before we jump into planning. Brian was a man of action; that was one of the traits that made him a superb salesman. But in resolving conflict, we need to move with prudence; we need to be thoughtful before we take action. Answering Question 5 motivates us to review our responses. In this way, we can go back and add and/or delete responses as we see fit to any or all of the preceding questions.

Achieving Balance

The Working Circle, as you know by now, is a balanced method of resolving conflict. That balance, between masculine and feminine perspectives, is very noticeable when answering Question 5. Asking ourselves how we feel in a work setting is, at best, an uncomfortable process for most of us. If, however, we incorporated it into our decision-making practices more often, we would be better able to balance introspection with action on a consistent basis.

The more thorough we are in addressing Questions 1 through 5 before we begin to develop our game plan, the more comprehensive the plan will be. That then increases our chance of facilitating a win!

One additional point here, before we move on: Brian, in reviewing how he felt about the situation, also reflected on the behavior of Bill and Erin. "You know, I'm annoyed at both of them for causing this situation. They really are acting worse than my kids," he said.

We both laughed.

After Brian made that comment, he paused again, then smiled. "You know, I actually feel good about what I have said so far," he said. "I'm ready to make a plan."

Question 6: What's My Game Plan?

Thanks to growing confidence in himself, Brian decided to attempt mediation. He had talked it over with his wife, too, who expressed pride in his courage, and agreed that he was right to attempt mediation.

What follows is Brian's plan:

- Make a list of his sales prospects and estimate how much he thinks he can sell in the next six months.

- Chart a breakdown of how much of his time he spends on prospecting, sales, and service. Give to Bill and Erin for the purpose of demonstrating how unrealistic their collective demands are becoming.

- Scope out a room at the site of the agency retreat where the three of them can meet in private.

- A week before the retreat, tell Erin and Bill that he would like to sit down with them together to discuss the very difficult situation he is facing. Stress the importance of the meeting, and that his goal is to make it a problem-solving interaction, not a confrontation.

- Take The Working Circle diagram with him to the discussion. This will be helpful to him in his role as the mediator. It should also be helpful for Bill and Erin, as they will be able to recognize it as a nonthreatening process for guiding their conversation.

- Take notes during the conversation, to ensure that all three of them will have a record of what was said, to help them adhere to the agreements they make.

- Bring a small gift for each of the managers, as a thank you for participating—something lighthearted, to make them all smile.

Brian summarized his objective for the meeting in this way: Increase sales results through a more efficient use of time and reduction of conflict. This objective was not intended to be interpreted either as blaming or complaining; Brian simply wanted to do the best for all of them, and they needed to understand that their conflict was inhibiting that goal.

Brian reviewed his plan, and then his answers to all of the previous questions. "I'm ready," he said to me.

As always, Brian was ready for action, so I had to remind him that he had two more questions to answer.

Question 7: What Transformations Will the Game Plan Bring?

"If you complete your plan, and mediate to meet your objective, what changes would you expect to see in the situation?" I asked Brian.

"Besides seeing them both [Erin and Bill] grow up and stop torturing me?" Brian asked with a smile, before answering more seriously, "I'd like to see them stop badmouthing each other to me, and most of all I'd like to be able to succeed with realistic goals and with realistic timeframes."

Once again I had to put the reins on Brian's desire to spring into action immediately. To do that, I asked him to enumerate the transformations that he thought might come as a result of his actions. Here is what he said:

- Have even greater confidence in dealing with conflict.
- Demonstrate to Erin and Bill that he was independent and could not be swayed to take either of their sides.
- Gain more mediation skills.
- Stop the constant criticizing.
- Be given the opportunity to succeed.

Finally, to rubber stamp the discussion, I asked Brian Question 8.

Question 8: Will These Changes Ultimately Be Positive?

Brian paused for a moment. "These changes will be positive only if the mediation doesn't backfire on me."

I understood his concern, but I also had complete confidence in Brian's ability to mediate with a good sense of what could and could not be accomplished. We completed the Circle and Brian began to put his plan into action.

The Mediation   To show how Brian worked the mediation, I will give you a summary of what transpired.

Following his plan, Brian asked Bill and Erin to meet with him at the retreat. He arranged for their talk to take place where they could be assured of privacy. He told his two managers that he wanted to talk to them about his performance, and working with the two of them. He was very careful not to criticize either of them or hint that they were doing anything wrong.

Bill and Erin agreed—although with some apprehension—to the meeting.

At the agreed-upon time and place, they all sat down—after some uneasy joking. Brian knew that his first words were critical.

So, before we go further into the discussion, let's first look at the Masculine-Feminine Continuum to see the contrast of possibilities for Brian at this juncture.

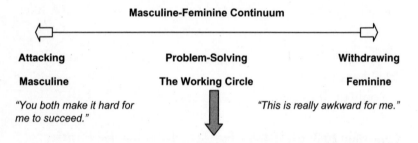

Masculine-Feminine Continuum

Attacking	Problem-Solving	Withdrawing
Masculine	The Working Circle	Feminine
"You both make it hard for me to succeed."		"This is really awkward for me."

Brian started the dialogue by taking a problem-solving approach, thereby setting the tone for collaboration:

"I wanted us to have this discussion because I want to succeed in meeting the goals set by each of you for me. Unfortunately, it is rather difficult due to the conflict that is going on between the two of you. I thought we could take a little time to clear the air, because if we don't, I fear my success is in jeopardy."

After a few comments from Bill and Erin—such as: "Of course I want you to succeed!" "I didn't know it was hard for you"—Brian introduced The Working Circle. He showed them the diagram and explained it was a useful tool they could use to help them discuss, without arguing. He asked for their agreement. Bill and Erin assented.

Brian stated that his goal for their conversation was twofold: to enable him to succeed, and to minimize the tension he was working under because of their conflict. (Note that he did not accuse either Bill or Erin; he spoke only for himself. That tactic enables collaborative discussion and problem-solving behavior.)

The three of them then walked through the questions of the Circle. Here is a summary of their findings:

Question 1. What's the Situation?

- Bill and Erin didn't like each other, but they both liked Brian.
- They wanted Brian to succeed.
- Times were tough, and Brian's dual assignment should last only until things got better—the economy improved.

Question 2. What's Negotiable?

- Brian could divide his time and efforts as he saw fit.
- Bill and Erin could determine how to handle their disagreements.

Question 3. What's Nonnegotiable?

- Erin and Bill would stop making negative comments about each other in Brian's presence. (This was a difficult one; both were on the defensive. Brian emphasized that the comments they had made weren't harsh, but they were unproductive.)
- Brian's failure was not an option for any of them.
- Unproductive conversation was not permissible!
- Results at the company had to improve.

Question 4. What Did I (we) Learn from Previous Experiences?

- Difficult times pass.
- Managers must do whatever they can to help their staff members succeed.
- Personal conflicts should be left out of business discussions.

Question 5. How Do I (we) Feel about the Situation?

- We can move on.
- We all want to succeed.   .

Question 6. What's My (our) Game Plan?

Brian was ecstatic when they got to Question 6, the game plan. Everyone agreed on the following:

- They would schedule progress meetings for the three of them, at which time Brian would give Bill and Erin the same data at the same time.
- Their meetings would also minimize the complaining that had been going on, and therefore would maximize the chances of Brian's success.
- The managers agreed not to be critical of each other in front of Brian.

Question 7: What Transformations Will the Game Plan Bring?

- We all will have a greater chance for to succeed.
- Brian will have a more manageable schedule.
- The tension between Bill and Erin will, perhaps, ease.

Question 8. Will These Changes Ultimately be Positive?

⚫ Everyone looked forward to the end of hard economic times, and believed that the agreements they had reached would make things easier until more resources could be hired.

One final note: During their discussion, Bill and Erin had touched lightly on their existing conflict, although Brian had not made that the primary issue. Now they acknowledged that whatever was going on between the two of them would probably continue, but they also agreed that Brian should not be caught in the middle of it any longer.

After the meeting, both Bill and Erin complimented Brian individually.

"That took courage," Bill said to Brian when they were alone.

Later, Erin told Brian, "My, my, you peacemaker! I like what you did!"

Chapter 8

Challenge 5

Deal with a Client's Anger or Allow Him/Her to Continue Shouting?

Some events in my life, although minor, have stayed in my memory because they were so different, striking, or dramatic. One such incident happened years ago when I lived in New York. I had gone shopping for shoes, and went into a small boutique shoe store in Forest Hills, Queens. I was looking around when a well-dressed woman, holding a leash with a poodle on the end of it, wearing a red bow on its head, walked into the store.

She was holding a shoebox. When the salesman walked over to her, she told him she wanted to return the shoes she had purchased. He told her he would be glad to take back the shoes and give her a store credit.

"Oh no, I don't want a credit; I want my money back," the fashionable woman stated firmly.

The salesman explained that he could not give her cash, only a store credit. The woman repeated that she did not want a credit; she wanted her money returned. The salesman then pointed to the sign next to the cash register, which read very clearly, that store credits only were given on returns.

The woman looked at the salesman, paused for a moment, and then said, "If you don't give me my money back, I shall scream until you do." The salesman looked at her, totally nonplussed. He assured her that he truly regretted her upset, but could only give her credit; it was store policy.

At this point, much to the salesman's—and my—astonishment, the woman began to scream at the top of her lungs.

"Okay, okay, I'll give you your money back!" the distressed salesman shouted. With her money in hand, she walked out of the store.

I share this experience with you as a dramatic example of a customer behaving badly, to introduce the challenge of how to deal with difficult clients. (I've often wondered if she ever went back to the store. I am sure the salesman hoped not.) Dealing with angry, hostile clients or customers, whether in a retail or any other setting, is definitely a test of one's professional mettle. It tests our patience, our customer service skills, and our ability to resolve a conflict, one we most certainly do not want to lose. Of course, there are some clients or customers we don't mind losing, because they are so difficult to deal with; but they are rare. In my 15 years as a consultant, only 1.5 percent of my clients have fallen into that category. For those, I chose to end the relationships, and was relieved once I had.

However, the lower one is on the organizational chart, the less decision-making power one has in dealing with clients. That makes handling difficult clients a particularly thorny issue for junior employees. Conversely, the higher up one rises on the corporate ladder, the more flexibility one has in deciding how to deal with those demanding customers. Also, for senior staff, the more painful the loss of a client is!

Meet Alberto

For this challenge, I will tell you about a medium-sized printing company in Chicago, which I refer to here by the fictitious name Ink Printing. The company is a commercial printer, whose customers range from large corporations to small business owners. The owner lived in Los Angeles, and had a number of other printing companies.

Alberto, a customer service representative (CSR) for the company, had worked at Ink Printing for six years. He had started as a printer on a large press and through hard work had risen to his current position in the customer service division. Alberto was good with people and enjoyed his CSR job. Primarily, he serviced the company's small business clients: graphic designers, museums, retail shops, automotive repair, and others. Whenever a print job was completed, he contacted the client to ensure that the client was satisfied. For the most part, the customers were happy campers but, needless to say, not all. So, Alberto attended one of my company's one-day seminars on "Conflict Resolution for Professionals." He was an active participant, taking many notes and asking lots of questions. He took part in the role-playing with gusto and, learned how to resolve issues professionally. At the beginning of the class, he had described how very uncomfortable conflict made him. But he left the session more at ease, as he now had communication tools and a process, The Working Circle, and so felt better prepared to address conflict.

Dissatisfied customers would contact Alberto via e-mail, telephone, or by coming into the office. Alberto's supervisor, Gina, was a relatively pleasant woman, who gave Alberto some latitude in settling customer issues. And because she was a very busy woman, she preferred that Alberto take care of many issues without involving her. Company guidelines allowed Alberto to resolve issues/credits and other problems to a limit of $500. Above that amount Alberto had to get approval from Gina. Alberto also had to complete prescribed paperwork, in detail and accurately, whenever he issued a credit or refund.

The client that caused Alberto much consternation was a hotel in the Windy City. Recently, the hotel had ordered 25,000 copies of a new brochure. The job had been completed and picked up the previous day, so Alberto added his follow-up call to his to-do list the day after. Before he got to the phone to do so, however, he got a call from the marketing rep at the hotel, who wasted no time in letting Alberto know how angry she was as soon as he picked up the phone.

"What the hell are you doing there at Ink Printing? Are you all idiots? The job is a total train wreck," the rep shouted into the phone.

This was not how Alberto anticipated the call would go, for sure!

Enter The Working Circle

The reactions I describe in this challenge took place in *very* short time frames, because Alberto did not have the luxury of sitting and reviewing The Working Circle and developing a game plan. He had to, literally, think on his feet, recalling what he had learned in my class.

"I am so sorry that the job did not come out the way you wanted. Can you tell me what the problem is?" Alberto asked.

"What's the issue? You should know! Don't you have quality control there? Doesn't anybody know what they are doing there? I have 25,000 pieces of crap, and I have an event in two days that I need the material for!"

Having someone screaming in his ear was the kind of conflict that made Alberto the most uncomfortable. To help himself, he grabbed his diagram of The Working Circle and glanced at the questions, even as the customer continued to yell at him.

"Do you hear me, or are you deaf?" she shouted.

Alberto quickly put into play what he had learned in the seminar about dealing with exactly this kind of situation.

When someone is agitated and angry, the last thing you want to tell the person is to calm down. That kind of comment boomerangs instantly. Think back on a time when you were excited or upset and someone told you to calm down. I'll bet you got more annoyed and, probably, angry at the other person. Instead, when another person is haranguing you, take this twofold approach: offer empathy and set boundaries. I want to leave Alberto's story for a moment to explain this in greater depth.

Attempting to problem solve while agitated yourself is virtually impossible. Likewise, trying to calm down another person who is upset is not easy. The most effective method to get another person to calm down is to demonstrate empathy. Yes, I know this is difficult to do, especially when the other person is yelling at you or being abusive, but it's critical to a successful outcome.

Know When to Walk Away

In situations where someone is acting totally irrational or threatening in any way, don't try to calm them down. Instead, head in another direction—away! For our purposes here, however, I am assuming that people act rationally most of the time and only lose it when they get upset for one reason or another.

Showing empathy in the face of conflict is one of the most challenging skills to develop. I certainly recall having to learn it, yet once I did, it quickly became evident how extraordinarily effective it was. To help you be able to show empathy, I want to introduce a communication tool called *active listening*. The key is to zoom in on what you believe the other person is feeling and then simply acknowledge that feeling. Don't admit guilt or wrongdoing; don't defend; don't attack. Simply, *acknowledge*.

If you reiterate accurately what the other person seems to be feeling, nine times out of ten, he or she will cool down— usually apparent because they will sigh, lower their voice, stop the verbal assault, and maybe even apologize (though don't count on it!). Most important, you must express empathy sincerely; it must not seem phony or rehearsed—sincerity is the key to success here.

Active Listening

For those readers who haven't been exposed to active listening, I provide here basic information from the seminar.

Active listening is:

- Assuring the other person with your words, tone, and body language that you are listening and have understood where s/he stands and how s/he is feeling.
- More than restatement
- An appreciation for the other person's opinions, even if there is no agreement
- Empathy, even if you are in conflict and vehemently disagree with the other person

Active listening is not:

- Caving in
- Urging another person to calm down
- Overlooking your own feelings

(continued)

(*continued*)

Examples of active listening:

- "It sounds as if you might be feeling . . ."
- "You are more than frustrated about this issue—is that accurate?"
- "You don't trust what John told you."
- "It is clear to me that you are rather angry about the situation."

These examples are just that—you need to use your style of speaking and language you are comfortable with, so that the words sound sincere, not canned.

Use active listening to:

- Obtain more information
- Help the other person reach a point at which he or she is able to talk calmly and reasonably.
- Mediate conflict among others or resolve your own conflict
- Defuse the situation

I want to reiterate here the two keys for successfully resolving a conflict with an angry person: *offer empathy* and then *set boundaries*. Active listening helps you do both, express empathy *and* let the other person know that he or she won't be allowed to speak to you disrespectfully.

Another communication tool, one that is highly effective in setting boundaries, is the *"I" message*. Basically, by delivering "I" messages you tell the other person what you need, want, or feel in order to move forward in the conversation. You let the other person know all this without defending, blaming, attacking, withdrawing, or even agreeing with him or her. You simply state where you are coming from and the result you are looking to achieve from the dispute.

"I" Messages

- Help people to say difficult, emotionally charged things without blaming or alienating others.
- Require the person delivering the "I" message to take responsibility for his or her reactions.
- Assist the disputants in clarifying issues.
- Can be used when you are in conflict or when you are mediating.
- Assist the disputing parties in finding direction toward problem solving, the key to conflict management.
- Reflect the speaker's needs and wants—"I need, I feel, I want."
- Do not refer to the speaker's perceptions about anyone else; "I" messages are about the speaker and his/her responses to what is happening and what has been said.

The easiest way to think of "I" messages is in terms of "I need, I feel, I want." You are telling the other person how you feel about what is transpiring between you. This is another difficult skill to learn, as our temptation is to tell the other person how *they make us feel*, as contrasted with how *we feel*. Here's an example of what I mean—I have taught this skill to kids of all ages.

Two 11-year-olds were arguing, and I was teaching them how to deliver "I" messages. I asked one child to tell the other how he felt.

"I feel that you are mean and not fair," he said.

I explained that those were not feelings; they were accusations. I asked him to try again.

"I feel bad that you did not give me a turn at the game," he then said.

Success!

Adults do the same thing: we think we are telling someone else how we feel, when in fact we are telling them how they *made us feel*. There's a very big difference. Once you tell people what you think they did to you, or how they made you feel, they have to defend themselves.

Let's say you were arguing with a friend, and the last comment she made left you feeling rather hurt. (Notice my language—I did not say "she hurt you.") You want to say something in response, and you also want to reach some kind of resolution. Consider the difference between these two statements:

1. "You really hurt me by what you just said."
2. "I feel hurt by your last comment."

The first response would likely aggravate the situation, because your friend would probably react by denying, attacking, or defending herself. The second comment simply states how you feel, not what your friend did. No one can refute what you feel; they can only deny what they did.

The key here: If you want to move to resolution, own your reactions. That increases the chances that the other person will own up to his or her actions and reactions, too.

It's also important to be aware that telling another person that he or she made you feel a certain way actually gives that person enormous power over you. *In a conflicted situation, you do not want to give anyone power over you.* Keep your power to yourself!

Let's put the two keys together—offering empathy and then setting boundaries when someone is being verbally abusive:

1. Express empathy—acknowledge how the other person is feeling.

2. Let the other person know what you need, want, or feel so that you can move forward toward resolution.

Meanwhile, back at Ink Printing, Alberto had just gotten an earful from the irate customer. He looked at his diagram of The Working Circle, and remembered the skills he had learned.

"Do you hear me, or are you deaf?" the disgruntled customer shouted.

Alberto now faced a choice about how to react. Let's refer to the Masculine-Feminine Continuum as a reference:

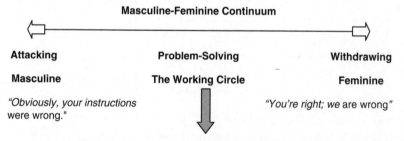

Masculine-Feminine Continuum

Attacking	Problem-Solving	Withdrawing
Masculine	The Working Circle	Feminine
"Obviously, your instructions were wrong."		*"You're right; we are wrong"*

The two critical aspects of this conflict are that the customer had a valid complaint, and that the customer was abusive, which is never acceptable. If, in a situation such as this, you react by attacking, you cease to be customer sensitive, and will make the situation worse. If, on the other hand, you react on the withdrawing side, you're essentially telling the customer it's okay to abuse to you. (In my opinion, it is *never* okay to let anyone be abusive to you.)

"Do you hear me, or are you deaf?" the disgruntled customer shouted.

Here's how Alberto responded: "I understand how upset you are, and I certainly want to take care of this issue immediately. I also need you not to raise your voice at me, so we can move ahead and resolve the problem."

There was a moment of silence on the other end of the phone. The active listening ("I understand how upset you are . . .") and the "I" message ("I also need you not to . . .") had the desired effect.

Alberto took advantage of the calmer moment to say, "Please tell me exactly what happened to your print job, and let's see what I can do to ensure you have what you need for your event."

Note here that Alberto still did not acknowledge any wrongdoings on the part of Ink Printing; he was problem solving.

The customer continued: "Well, in the first place, the colors are off. And in the second place, the folds in the brochure are not where they should be."

At this point it was clear that Alberto had effectively defused the situation enough to move into problem-solving mode. Again referring to The Working Circle, he moved on. At this juncture, Alberto did not have to go through the Circle question by question. The hotel was a new customer for Alberto's company, and he knew that it was nonnegotiable to lose the client. He also knew from experience that he had some latitude in resolving this issue, while also recognizing that there was a nonnegotiable deadline looming.

Here's how he proceeded—his game plan: He said to the client, "If you give me no more than half an hour, I will check the job, see what we sent to you, and look at the original order."

"I want it fixed, and I want it fixed immediately" the customer said firmly.

"I know you do, and I do, too." responded Alberto. "Just give me half an hour."

"Okay," she agreed.

Alberto hung up, and immediately did as he had promised.

As he ran down the hall, he ran through his responses to the questions of The Working Circle:

Question 1: What's the Situation?

For Alberto, there was one clear answer to this question:

- Ink Printing made a serious mistake with a new customer.

Question 2: What's Negotiable?

Here, too, a single, straightforward answer:

- In this situation, not much.

Question 3: What's Nonnegotiable?

Again, easy—to answer, that is, Alberto had to follow through!

- Completing the job, on time, correctly.

Question 4: What Have I Learned from Previous Experiences?

Alberto had a multipart answer to Question 4:

- Overcompensating, by providing exceptional service, a discount, and error-free work might help to salvage the relationship. Those tactics had helped in the past.

Question 5: How Do I Feel about the Situation?

A no-brainer for Alberto:

- Worried and hurried!

Question 6: What's My Game Plan?

Here, Alberto took the time to go into greater detail, to ensure no more mistakes would be made with this client:

- Get the job done right, even if it requires overtime.
- Get approval for a discounted price.
- Ensure that the delivery takes place no later than 1:00 PM the next day.
- Be there with the delivery, carrying a bouquet of flowers.
- Arrange for a postproject meeting with sales, press, and quality control to determine what went wrong and how to prevent it happening again. Note: Alberto was not looking to find fault; his goal was for everybody to learn, so they would not repeat the same error again. Blaming would only lead to defensive behavior and avoidance of responsibility. This point is extremely important when an error occurs at work.
- Follow up with the customer early next week to see how the event went, and mend fences.

Question 7: What Transformations Will the Game Plan Bring?

Alberto came up with three answers to this question, all upbeat:

- Ideally, no reoccurrence of this type of foul-up, but if there is, Alberto will be more confident he can handle it.
- Alberto will become even more self-assured dealing with difficult customers.
- He will become adept at satisfying customers.

Question 8: Will These Changes Ultimately Be Positive?

Alberto's response to this question was an extension of his answers to Question 7.

- I will continue to improve and enjoy my job, thought Alberto.

But, now, he had to make good on his promises to this important customer.

Within 25 minutes, Alberto called the customer back; he apologized again and then gave a timeframe for the delivery of the corrected brochures and pickup of the initial unsatisfactory ones. He also assured the customer she would be given a discounted price for the work, to make up for the upset and inconvenience. Ink Printing wanted to keep this customer.

Alberto was able to carry out his game plan, and the transformation occurred: the customer rep from the hotel was assuaged and the order was delivered to her the next day (at great cost to the company). He was there with the order and a bouquet of flowers. She was impressed with his service, and the hotel remained a client of Ink Printing.

Alberto was an excellent customer service professional. He took care of the customer: communicated internally what needed to be done, followed up as he promised, and took care of himself, as well, by not allowing the customer to abuse him. He knew that Ink Printing was at fault as soon as the client began expressing her dissatisfaction. But that didn't make it acceptable for her to yell and be abusive. Alberto had put his training to work very effectively, which was especially significant to him, as he was very uncomfortable with conflict and wanted very much to please the customer. He had succeeded both in becoming more capable of dealing with aggression and in pleasing the customer.

Chapter 9

Challenge 6

Get Your Boss Off Your Back or Continue to Be Micromanaged?

There are a certain number of questions I like to ask professionals when I interview them for a job. One of them is, "What kind of boss do you enjoy working for?" Without fail, among other things, every single person has answered, "A boss who isn't watching over me all the time."

Of all the managers I have met, interviewed, and worked for and with, not one has ever admitted to being a micromanager. Yet many of them were. Micromanaging is a trait that no one really likes or admires, so no one likes to admit that they might be guilty of this troublesome behavior.

One client I worked with, a manager at an engineering firm was, to my way of thinking, the classic engineer: very bright, very linear and concrete in his thinking, and very process-oriented. He decided he wanted his direct reports to complete weekly status reports. (I am of the opinion that much of what is contained in a status report is never read or necessary to include, but that's another topic.) This manager, Don, instructed his staff to report on almost every move they made. As it turned out, Don had instituted this practice because he had issues with one of his six staff members.)

I learned from Don's employees that they were spending approximately two hours each week preparing the reports. That meant 5 percent of their time was spent writing reports about what they were doing the other 95 percent of the time! Needless to say, they resented doing the reports, and had a hard time believing that every detail was necessary. In fact, Don often read them, and when he did, he would e-mail individual staff members with many questions, which required even more time to respond. Worse, when he was angry, he would write his e-mail criticisms in capital letters, the equivalent of e-mail yelling. Clearly, it would have been less time-consuming and more effective for all concerned if Don had given individual feedback to his one troublesome engineer. Then he could have asked his staff to prepare a broad summary, and ask questions for clarification when necessary.

What do we really mean by "micromanaging?" The term came into our language in the mid-1980s, when computers became prevalent in the workplace, and jobs and communication became more complex. Micromanagement is an attempt to control or to manage in excess—excessive detail and excessive control.

Why do managers micromanage, even though no one likes to admit it and no one wants to work for a micromanager? Here's what I think:

- Highly insecure managers are so afraid of failing they believe they have to closely monitor the work of their staff.
- Managers have staff members who are making too many mistakes or are highly undisciplined.
- Managers work in very punishing corporate cultures; no one is forgiven for making mistakes, and no one learns from them either. People are blamed and punished.
- Managers have bosses who are micromanaging them.
- Some managers think that they are just smarter than everyone else.

The dynamic between a manager and subordinate is complex, and very interesting. Managers typically want their staff members to be able to work independently, be productive, and make them look good. Staff members want to be provided with the tools they need to succeed, be treated with respect, be supported within the organization, and be permitted to do their jobs with autonomy.

How many managers have you worked for in your career? How many of them would you like to work for again?

In some ways, we rely on managers less than we used to in today's business environment. More and more professionals just want to be left alone to do their jobs. At the same time, managers serve as the links in an organization, connecting the top with the bottom, to ensure that the goals of the organization are being met.

When it comes to constructive conflict, there are some critical skills that managers need to have:

- The ability to rise above destructive conflict, using problem-solving skills, not judging or blaming.
- Compassion and respect for their staff.
- Mediation skills and as neutral a stance as possible in the treatment of staff members.
- Emotional intelligence—knowing how to resonate with others.
- Ability to give honest and direct feedback, both negative and positive, on a regular basis.
- The willingness to be introspective and honest about themselves.
- Ability to assign work and projects with clarity, avoiding redundancy.
- Knowledge of how to use rewards to support teamwork and healthy competition, and how to prevent backbiting among the staff.

Earlier in the book, I told you the reason I believe most people are fired is that they alienate too many people, not that they are lacking in skills. On the other side of the equation, I believe most employees leave their jobs because they are treated poorly, in one way or another, particularly by their managers. If a professional believes that his or her manager is disrespectful, dishonest, or demeaning, that person is not going to stay long at the firm. And if economic conditions or personal circumstances require the professional to remain, his or her efforts will be diminished, due to fear, anger, and mistrust, or all three.

When I work with professionals in conflict resolution, especially managers who also have managers, one of the major topics that cause great consternation is how to confront one's manager.

If you have issues with your boss, and you want to address them, one thing is of paramount importance: *Make sure you are doing your job, and doing it well.* Too many times I have met professionals who are quick to complain about their supervisors; they see all the warts on their boss, but don't see (or want to look at) their own. That is a major mistake! You must keep in mind that your boss has more power in the organization than you do. Your bargaining power increases exponentially if you have proven yourself to be a valued member of the team.

Here is the story behind Challenge 6: Get your boss off your back or continue to be micromanaged?

Meet Jocelyn

Jocelyn was a loan officer at a mortgage company in St. Louis. She had gone to grad school and earned her MBA, and had been in the mortgage and banking industry for 18 years, doing quite well.

Over those years, she had been through both boom and bust. For a while not so long ago, she had been making a great living, and her company was hiring new staff. More recently, however, the staff had been reduced dramatically, by 50 percent, and she was grateful to still be part of the team. Her income was not what it once was, but she and her husband both worked, earning satisfactory livings.

Jocelyn knew her stuff and did a good job, marked by maximum loan approvals and minimal errors. She was regarded as a valued member of the loan team. At one time she had managed a staff of six; now she had just two people, so more work and responsibility fell directly on her shoulders. She didn't mind, though, for she had a solid team, and she knew the business inside and out. She also was confident the downturn would not last forever.

Still, new regulations, high anxiety about the mortgage/credit market, regulatory agencies breathing down their necks all contributed to rising stress levels and sinking morale.

Jocelyn's new manager was Barb, a fast-talking, high-energy, take-charge woman. Barb had been the manager of another branch in the city until the corporate office had merged three offices and put Barb in charge. She was a tireless networker: she belonged to multiple industry organizations and was on the board of three nonprofits. She took care of herself, too, working out every day at the gym.

Barb and Jocelyn did not get along. Barb was a micromanager, and she didn't want her staff talking to senior management—that was her job. Whenever Barb came to the office (two to three times a week), Jocelyn felt sick in the pit of her stomach.

Barb's routine was to review the files of the loan specialists, sit down individually with Jocelyn and her peers, and grill them. Barb's goal was to increase the revenue for the office—

which was fine with Jocelyn, of course. The conflict arose because, according to Jocelyn's perception, Barb never trusted that Jocelyn was doing enough. It was one thing to be coached, Jocelyn felt; it was another thing to be dictated to.

Jocelyn, after all, was no novice; she had been in the industry 18 years! And it wasn't that she objected to suggestions—she could always use them—it was that Barb had a way of talking to Jocelyn that made her feel she had just gotten out of school. Barb would call Jocelyn and ask her the most mundane questions, implying that Jocelyn had made errors that she hadn't.

This kind of interaction was getting to Jocelyn more and more, and she began to feel trapped, even though she was aware that another mortgage company in town would probably be glad to hire her. But she didn't really want to jump ship at this time, as she also knew things were too uncertain at the other company. Still, she couldn't ignore the mounting tension between her and Barb.

Jocelyn had tried to ask Barb to back off on two occasions. On the first attempt, Barb acted astonished and dismayed. "Do you have something to hide?" she asked Jocelyn. That was a totally ridiculous question from Jocelyn's point of view, so she made light of the conversation and moved on, all the while seething inside.

On the second attempt, Jocelyn asked Barb if she trusted her. "Of course I trust you, Jocelyn," Barb responded. "Senior management has been dissatisfied with this branch's results, and that means we have to work together very closely." Jocelyn knew full well that senior management thought highly of her—they had told her so numerous times. She also knew that the results at all the branches were bad, not just hers. As a matter of fact, her branch was doing better than most. Consequently, Jocelyn concluded that Barb was trying to make herself look good at Jocelyn's expense.

Jocelyn walked away from that conversation more incensed than ever. She was now concerned about how she looked to senior management, in spite of the positive feedback she had gotten from them in the past. She was also concerned that she would blow up in Barb's face one day, something she really did not want to do.

Shortly thereafter, Jocelyn came upon Barb in *her* office, going through the files on *her* desk. That was the last straw.

Enter The Working Circle

Jocelyn was familiar with The Working Circle from attending one of my seminars. At the time, she wasn't sure how useful it would be to her, but now decided to give it a try. It was either conflict resolution or hara-kiri! Conflict resolution would be a lot less messy.

It's important to note here that when Jocelyn filled out the Conflict Styles Questionnaire, her score was 21, a mark indicating highly aggressive tendencies, and her primary response was to attack. Fortunately, she was well aware of these aspects of her personality, and was wise enough to recognize she had to avoid acting on them.

So, on a Saturday morning, while sipping a cup of coffee, she took out The Working Circle diagram, and began to answer the questions.

Question 1: What's the Situation?

Jocelyn took out her mental camera and took these snapshots of the situation:

- She loved her job, and no matter what anyone implied, knew she did it very well.

- She had a good relationship with her previous manager, as well as with senior management.
- Her loan numbers were always among the best in the region.
- She was infuriated with Barb.
- If she didn't do something soon to address the problem, she was afraid she was going to lose her temper at Barb.
- An important reason she wanted to stay at the firm was that she had some deferred compensation, and wanted to cash in on that before she left the company (if she eventually decided to leave).
- The situation was becoming steadily more untenable.

Jocelyn drank another cup of coffee, and though she feared the situation might be hopeless, she remembered she always told her kids that you need to try until you believe you have given your all. Now, she decided to listen to her own advice and continue answering the questions in the Circle.

Question 2: What's Negotiable?

This was a tough one for Jocelyn. Everything was so frustrating, and she was so angry, that nothing seemed negotiable. Her reaction isn't unusual. Often when we feel stuck in a very problematic situation, we think it's absolutely hopeless. It's important to remember at such times that we *always* have choices; they might not all be palatable, but we always have them.

For now, Jocelyn decided to skip this question and go on to the next one. Maybe after answering Question 3, she might be able to come up with responses to this one.

Question 3: What's Nonnegotiable?

This question posed much less of a challenge for Jocelyn, and she began to write furiously:

- Being spoken to and treated the way Barb was treating her was totally and absolutely nonnegotiable—and unacceptable!
- Defending her reputation was mandatory.
- She would not be pushed out of the company; if she left, it would be on her own terms.
- Jocelyn was determined to collect her deferred compensation; she had to wait only another six months.

By the time she finished answering this question, a few negotiable items came to mind, so she returned to Question 2.

Question 2 Redux: What's Negotiable?

Jocelyn came up with two items:

- Whether she would approach senior management was negotiable. She had a good relationship with two senior managers, and would feel comfortable speaking with them about the situation with Barb. But Jocelyn also knew that if she did that, and Barb found out, Barb would be furious.
- Working in another branch was a possibility she was willing to consider. The company had six branches in St. Louis, and Barb managed three of them. The other three were managed by another woman, Leslie, whom Jocelyn liked.

In going back to Question 2, Jocelyn began to feel a bit more hopeful—she had reminded herself that she had options.

She still had no confidence that Barb would in any way change her behavior.

The Working Circle, because it is a circle, allows you to go back and forth among the questions before you get to Question 6, the game plan. Jocelyn was making good use of the Circle.

She went on to the next question.

Question 4: What Have I Learned from Previous Experiences?

Jocelyn sat back and thought, rerunning various old movies in her mind. Suddenly, an experience that happened at her current job came to mind. Formerly, she had a loan specialist on her team (when times were good) who was well meaning, but made too many errors. Jocelyn wanted to give her an opportunity to improve, because hiring another person would be costly and time-consuming.

So Jocelyn started monitoring the loan specialist's performance daily. Soon, her performance improved greatly. Jocelyn continued to monitor her on a daily basis, until one day the specialist asked her why she was still checking her work that often: wasn't Jocelyn pleased with her improvement? Jocelyn acknowledged that the specialist had a point and reduced her checks on her work to a couple of times a week.

What did Jocelyn learn from that experience? To manage more closely when there are problems, and reward with greater autonomy when someone's performance has improved. She realized this could be an important point to make when she spoke to Barb.

Another lesson Jocelyn learned from the past was when she attended a conference two years earlier and heard someone speak on emotional intelligence. The topic intrigued her.

What she learned was that people perform their jobs more effectively when they feel they are trusted. Jocelyn did not feel trusted, and believed that if Barb gave her more room and a bit of trust, she would have a greater chance of succeeding.

These lessons from the past were helpful to Jocelyn, yet she still found herself going back and forth between feeling hopeful and hopeless about the situation, so she moved on to Question 5.

Question 5: How Do I Feel about the Situation?

This question was easy for Jocelyn:

- She was outraged at how she was being treated
- She was worried that she would lose her cool in front of Barb.
- She was not very hopeful that Barb would be anything but Barb.

"Okay," she thought, "let's see what kind of plan I can come up with." She poured another cup of coffee and continued.

Question 6: What's My Game Plan?

Because she felt mixed about the possible results, Jocelyn was uncertain where to begin. She was also being very cautious because she knew her temper might get her in trouble; above all, she wanted to act like the professional she believed herself to be. She didn't want to behave like Barb. Still, Jocelyn was aware that usually her first impulse was to attack, and that, she knew, would not improve the situation. It wouldn't help her deal with Barb, and it certainly wouldn't do anything for her self-image. With those thoughts in mind, this is the plan she wrote:

- Review her results and amend her projections, with an eye toward making more aggressive attempts to increase revenue (a challenge in this economy!).

- Ask Barb to have lunch with her. Meeting in a restaurant would increase the chances of their having an amicable, professional conversation.

- Relate to Barb the information about emotional intelligence she had learned (without making it sound as if she knew something that Barb did not) and how professionals thrive best in a trusting environment.

- Design a program that would incorporate Barb's need to micromanage and Jocelyn's need for greater autonomy. It would include less frequent formal reporting and more informal discussions on her progress.

- Ask Barb to respect her privacy and professionalism: if she had a question, she should ask Jocelyn, not rifle through her desk. (She would, she knew, have to approach this carefully, for sure!)

Finally, if her plan failed to achieve the results she wanted with Barb, Jocelyn intended to approach senior management and ask for a transfer.

As she reviewed her plan, she felt butterflies take wing in her stomach. This was not going to be easy.

Question 7: What Transformations Will the Game Plan Bring?

Jocelyn was very clear about this question, so answering it quieted the butterflies, and her anger at the same time.

- She would improve her ability to control her temper—something she wanted to do professionally as well as personally, with her family. This was the most important of all.

- She would put Barb on notice that Barb's management style was not working for her.

- She might be able to have a positive impact on her relationship with Barb.

Question 8: Will These Changes Ultimately Be Positive?

Absolutely! Jocelyn could either influence Barb to improve her behavior or she will ask for a transfer. Jocelyn thought that her positive standing in the company could assist in her efforts to influence Barb. And, Jocelyn thought as she finished her coffee, this challenging situation, together with The Working Circle, will make me a better professional, wife, and mother—if I can curb my temper.

Let's take a look at the Masculine-Feminine Continuum to see the range of choices available to Jocelyn.

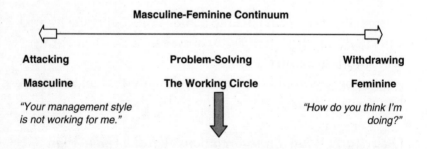

Jocelyn's normal style would have leaned more toward the masculine, attacking side of the continuum. (Remember that "masculine" does not refer here to gender, but to a conflict style.) Now, however, before scheduling the lunch with Barb, she thought and thought of different ways to introduce the subject of Barb's management style and the effect it was having on her morale. Specifically, she reflected on active listening and the use of "I" messages, and came up with a plan.

Think Ahead—But Not Too Far

When implementing your game plan, it's a good idea to decide what you want to say to introduce the conversation. But beyond that, preparing what you'll say is usually fruitless, because you never know what the other person will say or do in response to your opening remarks. It is far more important that you stick to your game plan, and maintain problem-solving language. It is counterproductive to try to figure out other people's words or actions. Remember: You have no control over them! If they act in a way that you didn't expect, you'll be thrown off your game plan and fail to achieve your goal—conflict resolution.

Two weeks later, Jocelyn saw her window of opportunity. She asked Barb to lunch, and though Barb looked at her somewhat quizzically, she accepted. At lunch, Jocelyn followed her game plan.

"Barb, I need to talk to you about how we work together. I have always been successful, and I certainly want that to continue. I know how hard times are, and how pressured you are. What I am asking for is that you trust me, and give me a bit more room than I have now to function more autonomously."

Barb put down her salad fork and stared at Jocelyn. "Are you telling me I crowd you?" she asked.

"I am not accusing you of anything; I just need to spend less time reporting my actions to you and more time working the program and increasing revenue."

Jocelyn paused, waiting for Barb to respond.

"You know, I have been a manager for a long time, and I know exactly what I am doing. If you aren't happy, that's not my problem," Barb said finally.

"Oh, no," thought Jocelyn. "This is what I was afraid of. Barb is intransigent, sees none of her shortcomings, and is totally unwilling to compromise." Jocelyn felt her anger heating up. But she managed to keep her cool.

"It's not about being happy or unhappy," replied Jocelyn. "It's about bringing in the results we both want. How about if we tried, for one month, this plan I have put together?" Jocelyn brought out her plan, which included what she would do and how often she would report to Barb.

"I'm the manager, and you really don't dictate to me how to manage," Barb replied angrily.

It became clear to Jocelyn at this point that Barb was jealous of her and that no matter what Jocelyn said Barb would have a negative response and deny her own culpability for the conflict.

Now Jocelyn faced a choice: "Do I continue this conversation?" she asked herself. "It is clear that Barb is becoming more agitated, no matter what I say, because she thinks I am challenging her authority. And I am getting more and more angry myself, and I don't want to blow up."

She took a minute to butter her bread before speaking again to Barb.

"Okay, I just thought that I could make life easier for both of us. I know you have issues galore, and I wanted to take less of your management time. Let's just have lunch." She managed to bite her tongue to keep from saying anything she'd be sorry for, then smiled and continued eating. It was a good move because the pause gave Barb time to get a grip on herself.

"You know, Jocelyn, you're a good loan officer," Barb said, "and I appreciate that. I'll look at your plan and get back to you. How's that with you?"

"Actually, that's fine with me," replied Jocelyn.

With that, they moved on to other topics and to finish their lunch.

Jocelyn waited for three weeks to hear feedback from Barb about her plan. It never came, and she vowed not to bring it up again. She waited another two weeks, then gave up hope altogether. Still, she was extremely proud of herself: she had modified her conflict style, had tried to institute change, and had followed her plan.

Now she continued to do so: she went to see the senior manager she liked and told him that she wanted a transfer. She did not mention Barb; that would have been counter-productive. (She did believe, however, that the senior manager knew exactly why Jocelyn asked for a transfer; he was a very smart man.) She said, instead, that there were personal reasons for the request. She also said that she believed she could bring new ideas to a different branch and in a slightly different market.

The transfer was granted, and Jocelyn moved to another branch two months later.

Whenever Jocelyn and Barb ran into each other, Jocelyn would smile and greet Barb in a friendly manner. "Hi, how are you" Jocelyn would ask—admittedly thinking all the while, "Who the hell cares?"

The lesson of this challenge is a very important one. Implementing The Working Circle does not guarantee that we will get the result we are hoping for, but we will gain valuable insights and experience. For her part, Jocelyn did extremely well: she matured as a professional and became a positive role model for other employees and her family. She eventually got transferred and received her deferred compensation. And, in fact, Jocelyn did facilitate a win-win: Barb got what she wanted, and so did Jocelyn!

Chapter 10

Challenge 7

Stand Up to the Bully or Don't Make Waves?

My favorite story about an employee facing up to an overbearing manager comes from a seminar I taught in Washington, DC, for a major accounting firm. There were 20 people in the class, made up of team leaders, administrators, and a few managers, and we were at the point where I was explaining to them the concepts of active listening and "I" messages.

One of the participants, Sarah, had been participating energetically throughout the day. She was a tiny woman, maybe reaching five feet in height, and dressed impeccably: tailored suit, butterfly pin on the lapel, not a hair out of place. She sat at the table with her back straight and her feet dangling, too short to touch the floor; she was very polite. She was probably around 50 years old or so, and she came across as a no-nonsense professional. She served as an administrative assistant for one of the partners in the firm.

I was explaining how to deliver an "I" message to someone more senior to oneself—an intimidating topic for the class. Sarah raised her hand to speak.

"You know, I work for a partner who screams at everybody all the time," she said. Everybody in the room laughed, knowingly, as they all could guess whom she was referring to.

She went on: "One day, I said to her, 'You know, I want to do a good job for you. I think I do a good job, and I could do a better job for you if you just wouldn't yell at me.'"

At that, as if they were one, all the class participants sucked in air at the same time, a clear sign they related to the fear associated with confronting a screamer.

"What happened?" I asked Sarah.

"Well, she still screams at everyone else, but she stopped screaming at me," Sarah said proudly.

The room broke up in laughter and applause. The story somehow seemed especially meaningful coming from this petite, mild-mannered woman. I complimented her on her courage and thanked her for her willingness to share the story.

As I've said before, bullies, whether they have organizational power or assumed power, can knock you off your feet, figuratively speaking. At one corporation I worked for, one of the senior VPs was meeting with a marketing director. These two did not particularly like each other. The senior manager was known to be an intellectual bully: no one could possibly be as smart as he was, and he let you know that in no uncertain terms. There were a total of four people at the meeting, and I knew that the senior VP was gunning for the marketing director.

"What school did you go to for your MBA?" asked the senior VP of the marketing director.

"NYU," replied the marketing director.

The senior manager looked at his cohort next to him and said, in front of the marketing director and me, "Remind me never to hire anyone from NYU ever again," then grinned widely. That is a quintessential example of a bully.

I'm happy to report the marketing director, after the bully fired him, moved on to great success elsewhere. The bully VP was also fired from the company, two years later. What goes around comes around. We're just not always there to see it.

An explanation of why people behave like bullies is the subject for a psychology textbook, not this one. Suffice it to say, I believe that bullies are born of insecurity, not confidence. I learned early on that the best thing to do in the face of a bully is to stand up to him or her, and not show any fear or intimidation. That said, it's important *how* you do that.

Courage is a running theme in this book. And nowhere else do you need more courage than in confronting a bully. And that's the purpose of this challenge: to exemplify what you can do when faced with an intimidator.

Meet Raymond

Raymond was a midlevel manager at a corporation (whose fictional name here is Mightier) that manufactured parts for the military. The company was primarily a government contractor, providing parts for all branches of the U.S. armed forces, as well as for several other countries. The company had three locations; Raymond worked at the one in Houston, Texas. He had been at the company for four years, rising up through the ranks quickly. A very task-oriented professional, he managed a team of 50 employees and 3 lower-level managers. His team was working on a number of different projects for the Air Force and Navy.

Before coming to Mightier, Raymond had worked for another government contractor, for three years, in California. Prior to that, he had served in the Army for 16 years, completing two overseas tours in two different war zones.

Raymond's manager, Charles, had nine managers reporting to him, including Raymond. Charles had been with Mightier for 22 years and had a good relationship with the SVP of operations in Houston. He had a degree in physics. Like Raymond, Charles was very task-oriented—his nickname in Houston was "King Charles," given to him because of his very commanding presence and practice of keeping everyone at a distance. Charles also had a reputation for being tough, and senior management seemed happy with him, as he made quality products and delivered them on time. As the expression goes, when Charles said "jump," everyone simply asked, "How high?"

With his military background, Raymond was very familiar with hierarchy, and knew how to take orders. But working for Charles was a different experience entirely. Charles would criticize Raymond to one of his other mangers, but not approach Raymond directly. Charles also would raise his voice at Raymond when he thought Raymond had made an error. Worse, though, and for reasons Raymond could not fathom, Charles seeming to enjoy chewing him out in front of others.

Still, Raymond tried to figure it out. Was it because he had gotten an "above expectations" on his review eight months ago? Yes, he had some problems but no more than anyone else. In the end, there were only two reasons Raymond could come up with to explain why Charles was on his back as much as he was: Raymond did not have a college degree, and was Hispanic.

If either or both of those reasons were true, then Raymond was really facing a difficult dilemma. But one thing he knew for sure, after having fought for his country, he was not about to be treated unfairly by anyone. At first, though, he felt stymied: he did not want to go to human resources; they were rumored to be useless. Moreover, he didn't want to be seen as a crybaby. So for now, Raymond did nothing, and Charles persisted in his attacks on him.

After one particularly difficult day, Raymond went home in a foul mood. His wife spoke to him.

"King Charles beat you up again today, honey?" she asked. Raymond growled a response. One of his kids approached him, and he spoke harshly to him. His wife stared at him, clearly worried.

"You have to do something about that man. He's making you miserable, Ray," she pleaded.

"I'm okay. I'll figure something out. What's for dinner?" Ray asked.

This pattern continued for another month. Then, at a meeting with an important vendor, attended by Raymond, Charles, and two of Raymond's peers, the vendor asked Raymond a question, but before he had a chance to speak, Charles jumped in. His remark to the vendor was filled with innuendos about Raymond's lack of technical knowledge and how the vendor should really deal directly with him. This was the final straw: Raymond did not intend to be belittled in front of an outsider, especially in regard to his education. He took a stand, then and there.

"I believe I am responsible for this project, and I will be the one you contact," Raymond said to the vendor, his eyes avoiding Charles. "Contact me as soon as you can with your information and specs."

Charles was clearly furious, and looked as if he wanted to jump across the table and throttle Raymond. His look said it all: No one countermands me, certainly not in front of others!

The meeting soon ended, with Raymond and Charles storming off to their respective offices. Within one hour, Raymond got an e-mail from Charles's executive assistant, telling him he was expected to appear before Charles the next morning. Raymond thought, "I'm done for."

After work that day Charles's behavior haunted Raymond and he found himself thinking about what he should have said. That evening, Raymond again went home in a nasty mood. When his wife asked what had happened, this time he told her. He also told her of the meeting the next morning, and that he was extremely nervous about what Charles would

Fight or Flight

When Raymond attended the "Conflict Resolution for Managers" seminar, he scored 38 (Compromising/Withdrawing). Raymond did not like conflict—more accurately, he *hated* it. He was a man who believed that, if you laid low long enough, most storms would blow over, so you usually don't have to fight. This characteristic served him well in the military, where he was known to be cool-headed when often others were not and so was capable of defusing volatile situations. That was another reason he had not gone to HR with his suspicions that Charles was prejudiced. It was also why he had never said anything to Charles himself. He had hoped Charles would eventually tire of demeaning him and move on to someone else.

say and do. His wife asked him whether anything from the conflict seminar he had attended might be helpful. (He had shown her the manual he had been given at the class.) He promised that, after dinner, he would look through the manual for ideas of what he might do.

When he came across The Working Circle, he remembered that, in class, it had made sense, but he had never used it after he finished the program. Now, he sat quietly and decided to follow the Circle and put together a plan for the next morning. He realized that if he didn't do *something*, Charles would just run over him, and his job (and self respect) might be in jeopardy. Not only couldn't he afford to lose his job, he didn't deserve to! But after the incident that day, Raymond was more sure than ever that Charles *was* prejudiced; he was also sure that such a charge would be hard, if not impossible, to prove.

Facing Prejudice

Raymond's story details a challenge that is extremely difficult to deal with. It is not uncommon for people to think that someone who is behaving badly toward them is prejudiced against them, for one reason or another. Sometimes they are right, and sometimes not. Certainly, prejudice is a source of conflict far too often in the workplace (outside the workplace, as well). This aspect of the dilemma only made the challenge thornier for Raymond, for in addition to being *highly* averse to conflict, he neither wanted to seek advantage because he was Hispanic, nor be treated unfairly because of his ethnicity.

Enter The Working Circle

Let's go through the Circle with Raymond.

Question 1: What's the Situation?

Raymond understood clearly the instruction to act like a camera as he reviewed the situation. Here are the snapshots he took:

- Charles consistently belittled, yelled at, and picked on Raymond.
- Raymond suspected that Charles was prejudiced against him because he was Hispanic and because he did not have a college degree, but he could not prove it.

- Charles was a well-established senior manager, and though he had the reputation of being very tough ("King Charles"), the corporate culture tolerated that kind of behavior.

- Raymond had acted out of character (and out of great frustration) at the vendor meeting, which had prompted the eruption from Charles.

- Raymond had been at Mightier for a little over four years, but needed eight months more before he became vested in the retirement plan at the company, a fact of great importance to him.

- For the past three years, Raymond's performance had been consistently rated "above expectations."

- Raymond hated conflict.

Writing down the last bullet point reminded Raymond how much he was dreading the next morning.

He continued on to Question 2.

Question 2: What's Negotiable?

In this particular situation, it was hard for Raymond to identify anything as negotiable. How could he possibly negotiate with Charles, who was more senior—and louder? He started to feel defeated. Then he realized working the Circle was his only chance. Besides, he had no other ideas, and he had to admit, even in his despair, so far it seemed like it might be helpful.

Focusing again on the Circle, he noticed that he could list more nonnegotiable items than negotiable ones. Nevertheless, he began to answer Question 1 and was surprised that, once he started to write again, his responses started to flow. Here's what he came up with:

- He didn't have to work for Charles at Mightier; Charles wasn't the only senior manager with projects like the ones Raymond and his staff were working on.

- He didn't have to deal directly with Charles about the prejudice issue. He had lived long enough to know not to question or accuse a person of bias, as he or she would only deny it, and the situation would only get uglier.

- Raymond had a friend at work, Ritchie, who was one level below Raymond and worked for one of Raymond's peers. They had lunch together sometimes, and hung out together at company functions; the two men and their wives had socialized on a number of occasions. Raymond liked and trusted Ritchie, whose parents also came from Mexico. The two men had touched lightly a few times on the possibility of Charles being prejudiced. Ritchie had no opinion, as he rarely had contact with Charles. Nevertheless, Raymond realized he could ask Ritchie for his opinion on how to handle the situation with Charles. Unfortunately, at 10:00 PM, it was too late to call Ritchie now. But he could pop in to talk to Ritchie early in the morning—if Ritchie were available.

- Raymond also had a cousin who was an attorney living in California. It wasn't too late to call her. She might be able to provide some advice on how to intelligently and prudently proceed with the discrimination issue.

- If Raymond intended to address the issue of prejudice, he knew he would eventually have to file a grievance with HR. But he also realized taking this action was negotiable, and this made him feel better, because taking such a serious step made him very, very nervous.

Very often, a person who is very uncomfortable with conflict has a hard time seeing where their power is in the situation. Answering what was negotiable helped Raymond to believe that he did have some options and—just as important—that he wasn't alone in his struggle.

Question 3: What's Nonnegotiable?

As noted, Raymond found it easier to come up with nonnegotiable items, which included that.

- Charles was not likely to curtail his negative behavior toward Raymond—that's just who he was.
- Raymond did not want to lose his job, in particular because he was only eight months away from being vested in the company's pension plan, something he desperately wanted.
- Raymond would not accept Charles humiliating or yelling at him any longer. However, he didn't know what to do to stop it.
- No one could diminish Raymond's pride in who he was. No, he wasn't as well educated as Charles, but he knew his stuff and did a good job. As for being Hispanic, he was proud of his heritage and the sacrifices his parents had made to give him a better life in this country.
- He could not go to Charles's boss with this problem, as they seemed to have a good relationship. For sure, he knew it would be tantamount to shooting himself in the foot if he approached Charles's manager behind Charles's back.

Mightier had a very formal culture, and company practice did not support circumventing one's boss.

As Raymond continued to list his responses to Question 3, he noticed he was feeling more and more confident. (Breaking down a complex and disturbing problem often gives one a feeling of empowerment.) And as much as he hated conflict, he began to see where he had opportunities for positive action. He also (not that he really needed to) felt more justified about doing *something* to alleviate this horrible situation.

Raymond moved on to the next question.

Question 4: What Have I Learned from Previous Experiences?

As soon as he asked himself this question, Raymond thought of an experience he had in Bosnia while serving in the army. At the time, he was a sergeant and two of his men were arguing: one was African American, the other Asian American. With raised voices, they were in each other's faces, no more than a foot apart. There had previously been some tension between the two, and it seemed to be racially based. While the shouting match was still going on, Raymond walked over to them and put his face close to theirs. In short order, Raymond success-fully defused the situation calmly, through humor. Both soldiers backed down, relieved that Raymond understood their perspectives.

What did Raymond learn from this memory? Two things: that he could stand up in the face of racial conflict, and that he could defuse a situation without raising his voice to the level of another's anger. He also realized that as much as he disliked conflict, when he had no choice but to deal with it, he was perfectly capable of doing so, by remaining calm and calling on his sense of humor. Racial tension was no joke, certainly, but humor could be used to defuse it, Raymond thought.

Another lesson he had learned from multiple incidents (mostly involving other people) was that the best way to silence a bully was to stand up to him or her. There had been much discussion at the Conflict Resolution seminar about doing just that: standing up to bullies. It surprised Raymond now that he had forgotten that notion—perhaps because he didn't want to be the person who stood up!

Question 5: How Do I Feel about the Situation?

"I'd rather do 100 pushups," thought Raymond, "than face Charles! I don't like it; I don't like Charles, and I'm angry at Mightier for promoting such a guy."

He paused and reviewed what he written thus far. And, he mused, "I'm ready to make a plan. I feel stronger and more willing to deal with Charles and his bad behavior."

Question 6: What's My Game Plan?

The first thing Raymond decided to do was to call his cousin, the attorney, in California. He reached her at home and told her his story.

"What do you think I should do?" he asked. She recommended an employment attorney she knew of in Houston. Though there was nothing he could really do before his meeting with Charles, he should at least contact the attorney, who would provide counsel about what he might do going forward. For now, his cousin agreed that it would be unwise to accuse Charles of discrimination at this point in time. She also cautioned him that he might be embarking on a long road to travel, but that it could also be a rewarding trip to take. For one thing, Mightier might not know that Charles was discriminating against Raymond, and if management discovered this, they might take appropriate action to reprimand and coach him. There were many possible outcomes to this situation.

Raymond wrote down the employment attorney's name and number, and told his cousin he would call her to tell her how things went. Then Raymond went back to his game plan, which ended up with these items:

- He would call the employment attorney.
- He would stop by Ritchie's office early in the morning and bounce some ideas off him.
- If Charles raised his voice to Raymond during the meeting tomorrow, Raymond would be prepared with an "I" message: "Charles, I can hear you really well when you talk to me in a normal tone. Yelling isn't going to do any good, so I'd appreciate it if you would lower your voice." Wow! Raymond could imagine himself saying words to that effect to Charles—though had no idea how Charles would respond. But, he reminded himself, that was Charles's problem.
- Raymond would ask Charles how he viewed his performance—what, if any, substantive issues did he have. And Raymond would ask for specific examples.
- Raymond would also explain about the vendor exchange from the previous day that had ended in the explosion from Charles. Raymond intended to tell Charles that he had a longstanding relationship with the vendor, and so truly believed that the dealer would be likely to respond positively to Raymond because of that relationship.
- Raymond also decided that he would, in some way, tell Charles that he expected to be treated as Charles's other

managers—that is, as an equal. This, he knew, would send a very loud message to Charles about Raymond's concerns.

Having a plan had always made Raymond feel more confident, and this one truly empowered him! He was ready for Question 7.

Question 7: What Transformations Will the Game Plan Bring?

Raymond had no hesitation in answering this question:

- Greater confidence in dealing with Charles.
- A strategy for addressing the suspected discrimination, thus giving the issue less power over his mood and confidence.
- Less angst in facing conflict.
- Potentially put Charles on notice that Raymond was not going to take his bullying any more.

Question 8: Will These Changes Ultimately Be Positive?

As Raymond prepared to answer this question, his wife came into the room, asking if he was ready to go to bed. He looked at her, and his thoughts moved to his children and his parents. The answer to Question 8 was a resounding, "Yes!"

Sometimes, as for Raymond, answering Question 8 isn't necessary. If you have done your homework, it serves an affirmation that you are moving in the best direction possible for you. You can think of it as similar to what a coach might say to a team as they leave the locker room: "Let's win this game!" Question 8 acknowledges your work, freeing you to implement your plan.

The next morning, Raymond caught up with Ritchie and briefly told him what was going on, and asked for suggestions. Ritchie assured him that he was doing the right thing. He had just heard a story that Charles had lost his temper at a meeting in front of a number of people. Others were saying Charles had gone too far and that senior management was "watching Charles."

That was encouraging news!

Before we follow Raymond to Charles's office, let's visit the Masculine-Feminine Continuum to scan the range of approaches that Raymond could make to assert himself.

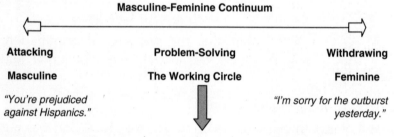

Masculine-Feminine Continuum

Attacking	Problem-Solving	Withdrawing
Masculine	The Working Circle	Feminine
"You're prejudiced against Hispanics."		*"I'm sorry for the outburst yesterday."*

"I need to talk to you about our working relationship."

Certainly the Attacking end of the continuum might feel good initially, but it would not accomplish anything in the long run, and the Withdrawing response would only encourage Charles to continue to be abusive; but there was plenty of middle ground to work with.

Raymond went to Charles's office at the appointed hour, but Charles kept him waiting 15 minutes. As he sat down, Charles glared at him. Raymond ignored the look and asked Charles politely how he was.

"You think you have the project we talked about yesterday under control?" was Charles's response.

"Yes, I do," answered Raymond calmly.

"Well, I don't, damn it! If you screw it up, we could lose the navy contract. What plans have you made to make up for the design flaw?"

Charles was growing visibly more agitated.

Raymond had come well prepared. He brought out his plans and gave Charles a copy. And for every question Charles asked, he had a good answer. Charles, Raymond couldn't help but notice, seemed almost seemed disappointed that he was so clearly on top of things.

At the end of the discussion, Raymond gathered his courage and asked the question he had prepared: "Charles, do you have any issues with my performance?"

Charles looked surprised, and then said, "Why do you ask?"

Raymond took a deep breath. "Well, it seems to me that you send a lot of criticism in my direction, and I want to do a good job, so I was looking for some clarification and feedback."

"No, no major issues," said Charles. "You could improve the quality on the navy program, and do it faster, but otherwise, you're fine."

"It was true," thought Raymond, "stand up to a bully and he has nothing to say." He pushed a little further: "If and when you do have issues with me, I'd appreciate your letting me know."

Charles now just looked at Raymond.

"And it would be helpful to let me know in private," continued Raymond. "I can hear you better then. That seems to be how you handle the other managers who report to you." Raymond was really scared now, but he had gone this far, and was committed to taking a stand.

"I'll let you know when I damn well please. Get out of here," Charles growled.

Raymond left Charles's office exhilarated. He had let Charles know he saw differential treatment, and he had been more direct than he had been in the past. More, Charles had acknowledged he had no problems with his performance— that would go a long way if and when the discrimination became a bigger issue. Raymond was proud of himself, and knew that for the first time in a long while he would go home that evening not thinking of what he could or should have said. He had said what he needed and wanted to, and not backed down! Best of all, Raymond had succeeded in producing a win-win result. It was a great victory!

Chapter 11

Challenge 8

Manage That Troublemaker or Let Him/Her Continue to Stir Up Trouble?

Without doubt, employees have been known to act in amazing ways—sometimes it's hard to tell the adults from the children. A few examples come to mind. The man who was fired for sleeping on the job and then came back the next day, asking to be rehired. The manager who refused to stop smoking in his office because it was his "constitutional right." Last (I do have a million of these!), the customer service rep who stormed out of her office crying because her manager had given her a reprimand. There is no end to how inappropriately some people can behave. It can take extreme self-control to manage such employees effectively.

Anyone who has managed employees has stories to tell about office intrigue, pettiness, affairs, jealousy, arguing, and so on. One client of mine, a rather generous sort, purchased special office chairs for two large-size employees. This prompted other employees to object: "How come they got new chairs and we didn't?" They continued to complain until, finally, the business owner succumbed to the pressure and bought everyone new chairs. This challenge is about dealing with employees who perform their jobs well but stir up trouble in other ways. They may think they are stirring the pot in a subtle way, but usually their behavior is anything but subtle! Instead, it tends to evoke conflict, and in doing so challenge management.

Here are some common examples of what I'm describing here: Troublemakers hint at possible wrongdoing of others, or they suggest that other people aren't pulling their weight, or they intimate that another employee is not loyal to the manager. Whatever the accusation, and no matter how ridiculous it may seem on the surface, usually the manager has to take time to assess the situation, to determine if any action is required and, if so, what is appropriate.

Senior managers learn early that everyone walking into their offices usually wants something. For them, they are in a continual learning process, in an attempt to sift through all of the requests and make good decisions for the business and staff. More seriously, when an individual is seen as actively trying to manipulate the leader to meet his or her personal agenda, the organization's interests may come at risk.

Being a manager isn't easy—the pressure is intense. Juggling multiple priorities and individual personalities within organizations that are in a constant state of change is daunting. Add to the mix that the workforce may be highly diverse, of various ethnicities and age groups, and from all over the world, and one gains appreciation for those who manage staff successfully. A manager, no matter how well trained he or she is, is never fully prepared for the peculiarities of human beings.

Here's an example from a university, where one likes to think highly educated individuals will behave in a civilized manner (how wrong stereotypes can be sometimes). Two professors were staging a protest against the department head (the manager). Why? The two professors believed that the department head was showing favoritism toward another professor. Their e-mails flew back and forth (of course, they copied the entire department), filled with animosity and vicious accusations. The department head was in shock, and at a loss at to how to deal with the bitter divisiveness that had developed. So there it lingered, eventually becoming part of the department culture—"Which side are you on?"

I tell you this story to introduce a very important topic: electronic communications (especially e-mail) and their role in conflict. As we all know, dealing face to face with a person you're in conflict with is, at best, uncomfortable. So, naturally, many think it will alleviate the tension to address the situation via e-mail. Wrong! When there is conflict, nuance, choice of words, tone, and body language, all become extremely important. What might be taken lightly in a normal interaction can become inflammatory when two people are at war with each other.

Interpreting tone in an e-mail is tricky; frequently, what the sender intended and what the recipient understood are two very different things. I learned early on that direct contact with others at work helps to build trust. The less personal interaction you have with others, especially those you might need to rely on later, the greater the chance that mistrust can build. This is not to say that you need to be in *constant contact*; no, what you need is sufficient contact to ensure trust. This is particularly crucial in cultures that are highly politicized, aggressive, or passive, where mutual trust commonly is at a premium.

Keep in mind that a lot of business today is conducted without the individuals involved ever meeting or speaking. Managers often have to supervise individuals who are not in the office across the hall, or even in the same building or state or country. Many people also work from their homes, and never participate in a corporate office environment.

Unquestionably, e-mail is a necessity in this complex world, where distance often separates people who rely on and work with each other, but it is best reserved for:

- Sharing of details of projects, plans, and the like.
- Distribution of announcements and news involving large numbers of people.

- Confirmation and restatement of conversations, agreements, and so on.
- Asking questions requiring clarification.
- Exchanging general communications.

On the other hand, electronic written communication is not effective for these situations:

- Any kind of conflict.
- Communication that contains emotional content.
- Privileged or confidential information.
- Personal or any nonbusiness-related communication (this should be on your personal e-mail account).
- Whenever the nuance of language is critical.

A client of mine, the regional head of a national corporation, showed me an e-mail he had received from the COO. The first paragraph (of many that were similar in tone and content) went something like this:

"DISCOUNTING ON CERTAIN MODELS HAS NOT BEEN DONE. WRONG! IMMEDIATELY, I WANT THIS ABSOLUTELY STUPID PRACTICE TO STOP! FAILURE TO DO SO WILL RESULT IN SERIOUS PENALTIES."

Oh my! We have come to understand that using all capital letters is the equivalent of shouting or screaming. Sometimes managing adult professionals has to be thought of as raising a family. You know what happens when you scream at kids on a regular basis? They become inured to raise voices and cease to pay attention. Employees react in exactly the same way.

If someone provokes you in an e-mail, don't react defensively. Instead, in a responding e-mail, let the other person know that you got the e-mail, but that you would like to discuss the issue over the phone or in person, whichever is more convenient. If the provocateur copied others in his or original e-mail, copy those same people in your response. Never forget, e-mails leave a corporate trail, and you don't want to be party to an argument that becomes documented in company records. Also, if you sincerely wish to resolve the conflict, you don't want the other person to misunderstand you in any way. Misunderstanding happens very easily when the conflict is being handled via e-mail. As tempting as it may seem to use this convenient technology, I strongly caution you against resorting to electronic means to resolve any issues you may have with another person.

Now let's get to the challenge at hand, the final one, another true story about an employee who causes trouble. Sadly, it's one that repeats itself on a regular basis in offices everywhere.

Meet Jeremy

Jeremy is a manager at a large food processing plant outside of Kansas City. He has been in his job for two years; previously, he worked at another processing plant in Baltimore. He is in charge of six supervisors (three men, three women), each of whom supervises about twelve workers. All these supervisors have been at the plant longer than Jeremy.

The plant functions well; productivity and quality goals are consistently met. Nevertheless, Jeremy does not want to be at this job much longer: he has his eyes on his boss's job. (His boss had told Jeremy that he would likely be his successor, when he himself was promoted.) His reviews have been excellent; he knows how to play the political game, and people generally like working for him.

The general perception has been that Jeremy is destined for big things in the company. His staff is aware of this, and most of them are proud to be working for a winner. For the most part, Jeremy feels good about his team; they work well together, and have few negative incidents.

One day at lunch, Jeremy and one of his peers were talking, and his coworker told him that their boss was probably going to be promoted and relocated to another location. Jeremy was thrilled. This could be the opportunity he was waiting for. With each successive day, Jeremy's excitement grew.

One morning, Nikki, one of Jeremy's six supervisors, and he were meeting in his office. Jeremy was listening to Nikki tell him how two of the other six supervisors were slacking off and cutting corners. Nikki also mentioned that she knew Jeremy was up for a promotion, and that this probably wasn't the time to be having production problems. She presented herself as being supportive of Jeremy. When he asked her for more information, Nikki told him that the slackers were also undermining her, making it harder for her to succeed.

Managing Staff Conflict

When managers are faced with a subordinate complaining to them of conflict with a peer, they tend to respond in a typical manner: "Tell me more." Well-meaning, often they attempt to work with the staff member who raised the issue, followed by speaking to the other person involved, in an attempt to resolve the conflict between

(*continued*)

(*continued*)

the two. Good intentions aside, this approach usually is not productive. Why not?

Once the manager listens to the complainant, others may perceive that he or she agrees (or is taking sides) with that person. Furthermore, by immediately stepping in to attempt to resolve the problem, the manager does not encourage staff to learn to resolve their own issues.

Therefore, I suggest to managers that when a staff member comes in to complain of a colleague, they say, "Have you spoken to him/her?" If the answer is no, then the manager should propose that that conversation take place. The manager should then add, "If you two can't resolve it, you can both come and talk to me, and we will resolve it together." It is the manager's responsibility to follow up, to ask how things are going, and find out whether the problems have been resolved.

If, after being asked whether she has spoken to the other person, the initiating subordinate responds with, "I can't talk to him—it's impossible," the manager should then say, "Well, let's call him/her in now and resolve it together."

Here are my guidelines for managers to follow when faced with one staff member complaining about another:

- Managers should not automatically attempt to resolve issues between subordinates.
- When listening to complaints, managers should, first, take the information, thank the person, and offer no opinions; second, state that no action will be taken until the other side has been heard.
- After sitting down with both professionals and hearing both sides, managers should encourage them to resolve

the issue between themselves, and offer to serve as mediator and ultimate decision maker. The manager should not be the person solving this issue.

● Managers should introduce The Working Circle as a process for the subordinates to use, to enable collaborative problem solving.

That afternoon Jeremy had scheduled a meeting with Tim, one of the supervisors Nikki had accused of poor management practices. He had to admit, what Nikki told him earlier in the day had stayed on his mind. He did not want to have any negative marks against him and his team, not at this time especially. Currently, the production stats were all fine. Jeremy was not sure how to proceed.

What happened next came as a total surprise to Jeremy.

At the meeting with Tim, unsolicited, admitted to Jeremy that he and Nikki were having issues. Tim also said he had heard that Jeremy might be up for a promotion (Jeremy wondered, *did everyone know?*), and hoped Jeremy would get the new position. Then he told Jeremy that Nikki was telling everyone that she was Jeremy's heir apparent: was that true?

Jeremy now saw that this situation was more than met the eye. He was well aware that as soon as there was a hint of organizational change, people start to jockey for position within the new regime.

Jeremy assured Tim that nothing had been decided yet; that it wasn't even clear that Jeremy's boss was leaving.

Then Tim added one more piece of information: that he had seen Nikki going out to lunch with Jeremy's boss the day before. "That is unusual," Jeremy noted to himself. He then promptly redirected the conversation with Tim from office politics to production issues.

Enter The Working Circle

Jeremy had come to realize that this situation was more complex than he initially thought, and that he had to proceed very carefully. After a week passed, Jeremy noticed that production stats were dipping a bit. He was concerned that the rumor mill might be directing attention away from the work. That, coupled with his ongoing concern about his conversations with Nikki and Tim, motivated Jeremy to go to The Working Circle.

Question 1: What's the Situation?

Jeremy surmised the situation as follows:

- Jeremy had staff members who were beginning to act in an untrustworthy manner toward each other, and potentially toward him, as well.
- His boss would probably be promoted—if not now, in the not-too-distant future.
- Jeremy wanted to be promoted to his boss's current position, should it be vacated.
- Nikki was jockeying for position and causing problems on Jeremy's team.
- Jeremy's instinct told him Tim had been telling the truth about Nikki, but he would have to investigate, to be sure—in particular, whether the alleged luncheon had taken place.
- Production numbers were starting to slip in Jeremy's group, an indication that employee focus may have shifted to political events, and off the production line.
- Jeremy had to admit he never completely trusted Nikki; he always had a sense that she told him what he wanted to hear, not necessarily the truth.

● Jeremy had not yet heard from the other supervisor whom Nikki had accused of collusion with Tim.

● If Jeremy did get his boss's job, he would not want to promote Nikki; he'd rather consider two other of his supervisors (Tim being one of them).

● Jeremy did not want his boss to recommend Nikki for promotion, for two reasons: he did not trust her, and she did not have a broad enough base of experience yet.

What tangled webs we humans weave!

Jeremy instructed his assistant to call his boss's assistant to see if she could confirm whether Nikki had had lunch with his boss the prior week. Within one hour, Jeremy found out that they had indeed had lunch. Now he was really irritated—and ready to move on to the next question.

Question 2: What's Negotiable?

The only item Jeremy considered negotiable in this situation was timing: when he would talk to everyone involved. He moved on to the next question.

Question 3: What's Nonnegotiable?

Jeremy had much more to say here:

● It was totally unacceptable to him that a staff member of his would have lunch with his boss without speaking to him first. It was, at the least, common courtesy, that she tell him about it.

● Likewise, it was not okay for his boss to have lunch with Nikki and not tell him—but this was a stickier subject, as his boss had a right to have lunch with anyone he pleased. Jeremy wondered whether his boss would tell him at their next scheduled meeting.

- It was unacceptable to him that his supervisors were allowing themselves to be distracted from their jobs and engage in backstabbing.

- He knew he should not be resolving issues among his staff members, that they should resolve things on their own—of course, with his assistance, if necessary.

- Since he had been told by his boss that he was his most likely successor, Jeremy expected to be told if that were to change, for any reason.

As it does for mostly everyone, going through the list of nonnegotiable items gave Jeremy more confidence to proceed.

Question 4: What Have I Learned from Previous Experiences?

Jeremy knew right away what his response would be to this question: At his previous job he had two team members who did not get along. He had spoken to each of them individually, going back and forth, trying to find a solution. But he never got a complete story from either of them, and the manipulation of facts ran rampant. From this, he learned not to get in the middle ever again. If people were arguing, he would mediate, assist them in reaching resolution, but not get in the middle.

Fortunately for Jeremy, he was not uncomfortable with conflict. He was also rather adept at swimming through political waters, which was an important reason he was so right for this potential promotion. What he did have a hard time handling in this situation was Nikki's behavior. Disloyalty and lying to get an advantage really got his dander up. It was that thought that led him to the next question.

Question 5: How Do I Feel about the Situation?

This is how he answered it:

- He was troubled by what his boss had done.
- He was mistrustful of, and annoyed at, Nikki.
- He was somewhat unsure of Tim.
- Most of all, he wasn't sure what his chances were for getting the promotion (if, in fact, his boss was moving up).
- He was very confident about his ability to put together a plan of action.

Question 6: What's My Game Plan?

Jeremy enjoyed planning, so he eagerly set about putting his plan on paper, and constructed on a timeline.

1. Call for a staff meeting with his six supervisors, with this agenda:
   i. Discuss the sudden dip in results, and determine how to improve.
   ii. Speak openly about the rumored departure of his boss, and tell them what he knew—nothing.
2. Schedule a one-on-one meeting with Nikki, for these purposes:
   i. Ask her how the lunch with his boss went. Also tell Nikki that he would prefer, in the future, to be notified of such events.

ii. Offer to meet with her and the two supervisors she accused of wrongdoing, If she refused, tell her that, in the future, she must have substantiation for any accusations she might make.

Let's interrupt his game plan at this point to go to the Masculine-Feminine Continuum and look at the ways Jeremy might handle the conversation with Nikki.

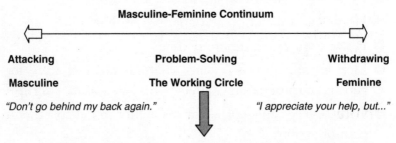

Masculine-Feminine Continuum

Attacking	Problem-Solving	Withdrawing
Masculine	The Working Circle	Feminine
"Don't go behind my back again."		*"I appreciate your help, but..."*

"I need to know that my team members watch my back, as I watch theirs."

Back to the game plan.

3. At the scheduled meeting with his boss, ask him the following:

    i. Was he leaving his current position?

    ii. What were Jeremy's chances of getting his boss's current job?

    iii. Was there anything he needed to know about the lunch his boss had had with Nikki?

4. If his boss was taking a new position, set up a meeting with the VP of operations, his boss's manager. At that meeting, express his interest in the promotion. If he got a favorable response, be prepared to suggest a successor for himself (most likely, Tim). Also, express his concerns about Nikki.

5. In the meantime, continue to monitor Nikki, to let her know he was on to her and was closely scrutinizing her production results.

6. Work with his supervisors, to ensure they were working together well and productively.

Reviewing his game plan, Jeremy felt great. He believed he had covered all the bases and was fully prepared to spring into action. He was also certain that he shouldn't give an untrustworthy subordinate too much room to maneuver; conversely, he didn't need to micromanage her, either.

Note

When approaching someone you have some misgivings about, it is wise not to ask "why" questions. Why not? Because when you do, you will undoubtedly get a "because" response. In other words, when you ask someone why, you will get a defensive or aggressive response. If, instead, you pose the question as, "What did you expect to get from . . ." or, "What brought you to . . . ," the answers you get will contain more usable information, not just a defensive argument.

Jeremy asked himself the next question on the Circle.

Question 7: What Transformations Will the Game Plan Bring?

He was confident his game plan would result in the following:

- He would reestablish his relationship with his staff, which seemed a bit offtrack now. The way he liked it to be is marked by direct conversation with honest feedback.
- Nikki would be on notice that certain kinds of behavior were unacceptable to him.
- He would feel more in control of his team.
- He would be more prepared for greater responsibility.

Jeremy believed his plan would enable him to move in the direction he wanted to go. It would position him well for the promotion and, in the meantime, help him to align his allies and put his adversaries (notably, Nikki) on notice.

Question 8: Will These Changes Ultimately Be Positive?

Jeremy knew that control was an illusion; but he also knew that this situation taught him how to deal with a number of important issues, thereby making him a better manager and professional.

When Jeremy met with his boss, it became clear that he was moving up the corporate ladder and that Nikki had spontaneously joined him for lunch. He also recognized that his boss was not impressed with Nikki's efforts at manipulation, a great relief to Jeremy. Most important, his boss confirmed that he had recommended Jeremy to take his place, and encouraged Jeremy to sit tight for a while.

Three months later, Jeremy was promoted, and, in turn, promoted Tim. "Now Nikki is your problem," Jeremy joked with Tim at a celebratory lunch they had together.

The Eight Challenges: Summary

Is there always so much conflict at work? Well, yes and no. Some conflicts are so small they barely register, like one mosquito at a picnic. Others are more persistent, like a dull, chronic toothache. And a few just drive you crazy—like an older brother who behaves like a typical older brother. Oh my!

On a personal note, I want to say that I try really hard to walk my talk, and I do that best by sharing with others The Working Circle. And I can promise you, The Working Circle works.

Note

You don't have to memorize The Working Circle. Simply make a copy of the diagram from this book and keep it handy.

My goal is for organizations to thrive and for people to enjoy working at them and to feel valued. In the next chapter, I will explain how you can help in this effort, by spreading the word and teaching others to use The Working Circle.

Chapter 12

Teaching Others Without Being a Teacher

Introducing The Working Circle at Work

Once you change your behavior, it takes practice to maintain it and then improve further. It is especially hard when those around you seem to be exhibiting the same behavior as always. It was Mahatma Gandhi who told us that we must be the change we want to see in the world.

Therefore, I recommend you take The Working Circle to work. At first, you can even do this under the radar. Demonstrating new, positive behavior before you try to teach others increases the chances that they will change, too. No matter what your conflict resolution style is, you can become a problem solver, as opposed to a problem maker. Being a problem solver makes you independent, professional, and in demand. And being in demand means that you will have more and better choices relating to your career. In good times, you will reap outstanding benefits; in hard times, you are more likely to remain employed. And, once employed, to get the job and the rewards you deserve.

I want to expand on what I mean by taking the Circle to work under the radar. That is, don't broadcast the Circle; instead, use it. Use the questions as a way to open new perspectives from which to examine issues. Use the language—in particular, the terms "negotiable" and "non-negotiable." Introduce the concept of learning from the past (Question 4)—but note, do this with caution. Here are some examples of how you can ask this question without alienating others:

- "Before we move forward, I think it might be helpful to take a look at the lessons we've learned from past experiences, good and bad." Note that I did not use the words "errors" or "failures." No one will volunteer to discuss their failures, past or present.

- If someone is being negative about a plan or suggestion, and says something along the lines of, "We tried that before and it didn't work," ask the person to relate what lessons were learned from that failure that might be helpful to the current problem.

- Start the discussion about past experiences and their lessons by relating one of your own. This can go a long way toward setting the new tone, that of learning from the past, and perhaps, help those involved move away from blaming behavior and/or avoiding responsibility.

Don't be tempted to skip Question 5 ("How do I/we feel about the situation?"), as in answering it you can determine whether or not further discussion needs to happen before solutions are proposed. At the same time, especially if your culture is a masculine-oriented one, don't dwell on this question, as it may be viewed as weakness to discuss emotions within the context of a business issue (even though we know emotions affect all conflicts).

Work hard at avoiding jumping to Question 6 (What's my game plan?) before sufficient discussion has taken place. This is the number-one error people make when attempting to resolve issues.

When I think about my greatest teachers, I remember that what so impressed me is that they led by example, not by lecture. In the same way, by using The Working Circle, along with changing your language, both verbal and body, you will become a role model for others. Just this morning I spoke to a client, a senior manager, covering issues related to a manufacturing operation. More than anything else, we talked about two men at his company, one a positive role model and the other someone who regularly alienates people. The senior manager revealed to me that he had learned to circumvent the alienator, because he had given up expecting to get cooperative behavior from this man. That avoidance tactic can only have a negative impact on the operation and the management team. My wish is that The Working Circle will help managers minimize the negative influence of the alienators.

By now, I suspect that certain aspects of the Circle have had a greater effect on you than others. Use those parts first in introducing the Circle at work. Then, when you are more comfortable, come back to the book and pick a challenge and review the key elements in it. I am sure you will find doing this helpful.

Take the time to review the concepts of "I" messages and active listening: those skills have saved me more times than I can count. Practice with someone you like and feel safe with, at home or at work. I mentioned earlier that I have taught The Working Circle to children, starting at age twelve; your children will benefit from it, and you will reinforce your learning.

I also recommend that you practice your new conflict resolution skills in your personal life. (I feel another book coming on!) No one can push our buttons more powerfully than family members. Because they have known us our whole lives, our families assume that our conflict resolution style is what it is, and will never change. Therefore, the temptation to act in our old ways with our families is often overpowering. Practice being a problem solver with your family!

Over the last 14 years since I began using the Circle, I have walked in my backyard, starting at the eastern perimeter, asking the eight questions. As I ask and then answer each question, I continue to walk, until I have covered all the questions. This practice has proven to be of great benefit to me and I recommend it highly.

What if Your Work Environment Rewards Win-Lose Behavior?

Changing your behavior is a challenge, no doubt about it, and doing it is much more difficult if the environment you work in doesn't support the change. It is still possible to accomplish, but usually must be carried out in smaller increments. Here's an example: a coaching client of mine who worked in a high-tech company decided to modify her conflict resolution style. She wanted to become more of a problem solver, because she believed that would accelerate her career. She took my suggestions and used her personal life as her laboratory before she began implementing the Circle at work, where the culture leaned heavily on the masculine side of the continuum. She knew she had to proceed carefully, to ensure she would be perceived as a problem solver, not a problem maker. Her fear was that by giving up some of the masculine behaviors she had developed to fit in, she might fall out of step with the culture.

She incorporated active listening and adapted the use of "I" messages to her language, which included expletives when she thought it was fitting; but she stopped directing the cursing *at* others, and used those words only as adjectives. (Note: The use of expletives and other colorful language is an accepted norm in many corporate cultures.) In this way, she was seen as still part of the culture, but she was no longer using such language to attack.

She took five other actions to ensure that her Everybody Wins approach was successful:

1. When speaking about her accomplishments, she began substituting the pronoun "we" for "I." She managed a team whose members helped to make her look good, and she wanted to maintain their loyalty and to demonstrate teamwork. She also wanted to show appreciation to her team!

2. She maintained an assertive stance while still being collaborative. (Her score on the Conflict Resolution Questionnaire had been 24.) Together, she and I worked on being assertive while learning to show appreciation for others.

3. She actively sought the opinions of others, which goes a long, long way toward ensuring a win-win environment. Masculine cultures don't typically support this behavior.

4. She committed to letting other people finish speaking before she started. Not interrupting is definitely a challenge in a masculine culture!

5. She maintained her focus on the transformation she wanted to take place in herself—she's a very task-oriented person, so keeping her eye on the prize kept her motivated.

After she accomplished these objectives, she introduced The Working Circle to her team. As a result, destructive conflict among them was greatly reduced and creative solutions to problems increased.

In contrast with that client, another coaching client of mine worked in a personal service company that was high on the feminine side of the continuum. Conflicts were avoided. When someone did not think a meeting was important, or was being chaired by an adversary, he or she found some excuse for not attending. My client liked his job and wanted to remain at the company, but he was going nuts in this environment of noncommunication. With everyone avoiding direct communication and/or hurting people's feelings, recurring conflicts never got addressed and problems never got resolved. Instead, the office atmosphere was marked by divided camps, lots of gossip, inadequate information, and a lack of creative problem solving. A bubble of stagnation surrounded the company, and my client wanted to burst it.

After he had the opportunity to learn The Working Circle, and came to feel at ease with it, he put together this plan for change:

1. Speak to his manager, discuss his plan, and seek support for its implementation. My client's behavior had been changing for the better, and his manager was well aware of the new positive outlook. (An important factor here is that my client's manager had been part of the coaching process, and so he had an advocate.)

2. He would use The Working Circle to mediate conflicts existing among members of his team, helping them to become more comfortable with conflict and the nonconfrontational resolution process.

3. Introduce some of the Circle's concepts to his peers (especially learning from past experiences and negotiable and nonnegotiable perspectives).

4. Choose two peer allies whom he could trust. Explain what he was trying to do (the culture made them uncomfortable, too, but they had not had the courage yet to take any steps

to change things.) After he gained their support, they could all make adjustments to their language and conflict resolution processes.

5. Speak to the HR director and request that a conflict resolution class using The Working Circle be introduced at the company, starting with the senior management team.

It is interesting to note that the transformation was more challenging in this feminine culture than at the more masculine-oriented tech company. The managers here thought that dealing directly with conflict would cause hurt and be rude. It took some time for my client to demonstrate, through his own behavior, that resolving conflict did not have to be discourteous. Ultimately, my client had a modicum of success within his sphere of influence, although the company culture at large did not change, a corner of it did.

What Should You Realistically Expect if You Work for a Problem Maker?

By reviewing the stories in this book, learning about the different conflict resolution styles, and exploring the experiences of your own life, you should have a thorough understanding of the various types of problem makers found at many workplaces. You also know by now that your new outlook and new way of approaching conflict will not change things at work overnight.

I speak from experience. I can attest to the changes I have seen take place, in my own style and work life. I used to think that people really wanted to hear all the things I had to say about how they had acted poorly, especially toward me. I usually had to have the last word. In matters of the heart,

I would shut down, and walk away silently carrying my wounded heart in my hands. I learned that neither approach was productive, for me or for my relationships.

I developed The Working Circle, in part, because I needed it, for I believe that we teach what we need to learn. Now I am a very effective negotiator, using my process to get my needs and wants met. These days, as well, I have very few arguments with others because I know how to defuse problems before they escalate. Best of all, with all this practice, I can say even the most difficult things with ease and compassion, and still get my message across effectively.

My point here is that there will always be problem makers, but I don't have to buy into their behavior, and I certainly do not have to act like they do. Neither do you. Most of us spend more of our time with people at work than we do with our friends and families. We might as well make it work well! If we wait for the other guy to change, we will grow old quickly.

What can you expect if you incorporate the lessons of this book with The Working Circle? *Incremental change*, which is less chaotic and longer lasting. You also can expect a small change in an existing conflict, followed by no change for a while. Then, when another potential unpleasant situation comes up, you will be better prepared to handle it in a way that serves you well and allows everyone to win.

One of the most telling examples took place here in Tucson a number of years ago. The client I was working with had cowboys working for him—and I mean real cowboys. I was, at the time, a relative newcomer to Tucson, fresh from big-city corporate cultures. This business leader wanted me to resolve issues among a group of employees who wore cowboy hats, rode horses, and towered over me. I knew that most, if not all of these men, owned guns, and had used them for one reason or another. They came from Arizona, South Dakota, and other states that were, to me, only images from television scenes I watched when I was living in an apartment building in New York City.

The business owner was a cowboy himself: tall, handsome, smart, and a no-nonsense kind of man. He and I were on opposite ends of the political spectrum; whenever we discussed politics, we disagreed. Nevertheless, he saw the value of conflict resolution, because destructive conflict was eroding his profits.

I taught his staff The Working Circle, and used it every chance I had. Slowly, the threats and the intense blaming behavior shifted. The company incorporated The Working Circle into its performance appraisals. And while some of the more negative employees left or were fired, those remaining learned that the old behavior was no longer acceptable and changed to accommodate the new approach. The business owner and I continued to disagree on many things, including about solutions to social issues; but we agreed on something much more important: basic human values. I'm proud to say he and his wife became my friends.

The numerous examples I provide in this book demonstrate that no matter what the culture, no matter what the situation, you can effect change—change in yourself, thereby generating change in your environment, like the ripples on a lake.

If you work for a problem maker, you have choices:

1. Do you want to continue to work there?
2. If no, start looking!
3. If yes, be consistent in your behavior. Become a respected problem solver. Use collaborative language and all of the

other tools at your disposal, including The Working Circle.

4. Be patient, be consistent; make allies. Do a great job.

5. Focus on the transformation you want to see in yourself and let others take care of themselves, even that problem-maker manager!

I know you can do it. I have seen it happen countless times. If you keep wishing the problem maker would change, I assure you it would be more productive to believe that you will win the lottery.

Epilogue
"Working the Circle" as You Advance Your Career

If we divided our careers into sections, those sections might look something like this:

1. Getting started
   - Landing the first job
   - Learning the system
   - Exploring different environments, people, and positions
   - Developing a view—probably somewhat unrealistic at this stage—of one's strengths and weaknesses
   - Hungering for feedback
   - Feeling intimidated by, yet wanting to be among, senior management
   - Developing organizational loyalty

2. Building the résumé
   - Finding greater autonomy
   - Feeling some disillusionment with the system
   - Accomplishing successful project management
   - Developing allies and adversaries
   - Gaining deeper insight into one's strengths
   - Gaining greater awareness of one's weaknesses
   - Still desiring feedback, but lower expectations of getting it
   - Feeling diminished organizational loyalty
3. Gaining competence (Note: This usually implies you've had two or three jobs by now, though not necessarily)
   - Having less reliance on feedback
   - Gathering leadership opportunities
   - Defining preferences for environments, people, and positions
   - Moving up the organizational chart (if that has been a goal)
   - Achieving greater financial independence
   - Experiencing, perhaps, being laid off or even fired
   - Growing skepticism toward senior management
   - Taking pride in one's strengths, concern about one's weaknesses
   - Having loyalty to oneself and one's manager (if he or she is a positive role model), as opposed to the organization
4. Focusing on the 401(k)
   - Not needing feedback
   - Having less patience for those who don't do their jobs
   - Listing multiple accomplishments on one's resume

- Developing a somewhat distorted view of oneself, if one has reached senior management at this juncture
- Desiring meaningful challenges without interpersonal complications
- Positioning oneself to serve as a mentor to others
- Acknowledging that the relationship between employers and employees is adversarial
- Accepting that the organization is a job provider, a vehicle to financial freedom, nothing more, nothing less
- Taking pride in one's accomplishments and relationships built over time

How does The Working Circle link to these four phases? The chart here shows how the Circle can be effectively implemented during each phase of your career.

In Conclusion

Is there always so much conflict at work? Well, yes and no. Some conflicts are so small they barely register, like one mosquito at a picnic. Others are more persistent, like a dull, chronic toothache. And a few just drive you crazy—like an older brother who behaves, well, like a typical older brother.

> **Note**
>
> You don't have to memorize The Working Circle. Simply copy the diagram from this book and keep it handy.

My goal for this book and through my seminars and classes is to help organizations thrive and for people to enjoy their jobs and to feel valued. I try really hard to walk my talk, and I do that best by sharing with others The Working Circle. And I can promise you, The Working Circle works.

Four Career Phases

Career Phase	Coworkers	Management	Staff	Customers
Getting started	Adapting to the world of work Becoming a team player Learning how to be chosen for winning teams Learning how to be rewarded	Demonstrating that you are on their team Doing your job well and work within the system Showing initiative, consistently cultivating skills/expertise	If you have staff (you may not yet), following policies and procedures without alienating others	Being likable and assertive Results oriented Willing to go the extra mile
Building the résumé	Informal leadership among your peers Reliable, honest, collaborative, communicative	Showing your potential for more rewards Eager to do what is needed Willing to raise questions and concerns professionally	Becoming someone others want to work for Serving as buffer between staff and senior management	Beating the competition with stellar service Improving methods to improve results
Gaining competence	Becoming the "go-to" person Cross-department leadership	Broad-based management Choice assignments and rewards	Managing for outstanding results Easy to recruit staff	Customers are loyal to you and your team
Focusing on the 401(k)	Developing true collegiality Sharing knowledge and support	Understanding that management needs support from the troops Developing successors	Appreciating good work and effectively dealing with poor work	Developing long-standing relationships with customers

Sources

I decided to return to school to earn my PhD while I was still working in the corporate world. I chose Union Institute & University, because the school encouraged interdisciplinary studies. My passion for conflict resolution began when I was a child, and only grew stronger as I became an adult.

For the design and development of The Working Circle, I used a tremendous number of sources. I went outside the norm for my studies, as there were very few PhD candidates focusing on conflict resolution in 1993. As you read on, I expect that the ingredients for The Working Circle might surprise you; I assure you, they transformed both me and my work. I include them here so that you can better understand the richness of The Working Circle, and why it is so effective.

The ingredients of The Working Circle are as follows, along with explanations of how each component contributed to the end product:

Conflict Resolution Theory and Practice

I was introduced to the field of conflict resolution when I earned my Masters in Organizational Psychology from

Columbia University, Teachers College. One day, Dr. Morton Deutsch, one of the "fathers" of the field, gave a guest lecture, and I was enthralled. His talk demonstrated to me that there was a field of study that matched my passion. But I was just entering the corporate world, to test my competitive mettle, and so that passion would go underground and not surface again until my last corporate position, 12 years later.

The field that captured my attention was transformative conflict resolution, as defined by Robert A. Baruch Bush and Joseph P. Folger, in 1994, who described two goals arising from conflict: resolution and personal transformation. In their book, *The Promise of Mediation: Responding to Conflict Through Empowerment and Recognition* (Jossey-Bass, 1994), they wrote, "In the transformative orientation, the ideal response to a conflict is not to solve the 'problem.' Instead, it is to help transform the individuals involved . . ."

Social Psychology

The study of how groups behave has always been fascinating to me. The areas of decision making, group influence, and so on were all critical to my work, and the work of I. L. Janis was at the top of my list. *Groupthink*, a term coined by Janis, occurs when a group makes faulty decisions because group pressures lead to a deterioration of "mental efficiency, reality testing, and moral judgment."[1]

Adult Learning Theory

How adults learn became another knowledge component that I needed for my studies. If I wanted to be able to teach adults

---

1. Janis, Irving L. 1972. *Victims of Groupthink* (New York: Houghton Mifflin), p. 9.

how to resolve conflict and to transform, I needed to understand under what circumstances adults learn best.

The Native American Medicine Wheel

It seems that most tribes indigenous to North and South America used some form of the Medicine Wheel in their cultures. I studied the Medicine Wheel with Rosalyn Bruyere, a medicine woman and healer, living in California. Her book, *The Sacred Medicine Wheel Workbook*[2] was a valuable source for me.

"The Medicine Wheel," Bruyere wrote, "is a practical system for maintaining a balance of power among all tribal peoples. It was the knowledge that no one lodge, no one tribe, could hold all the power which kept native people living in harmony here on Turtle Island (i.e., North America) for thousands of years before the coming of the White Man. When this nation was formed, the six Iroquois Nations taught the Wheel to our Founding Fathers, most notably Thomas Jefferson, and it is based upon these teaching that our government's system of checks and balances was originally based."

I recognized that the basic structure and layout of the Medicine Wheel, as opposed to the traditional linear processes so often used in conflict resolution, would allow for a journey of perspectives.

Buddhism

During my doctoral studies, I attended many individual sessions with Lopon Claude D'Estree, at the time the Buddhist

2. Bruyere, Rosalyn. 1992. *The Sacred Medicine Wheel Workbook* (Sierra Madre, CA: Bon Productions).

chaplain at the University of Arizona. I learned that compassion had to be the foundation of all of my actions. Buddhism teaches that we need to be compassionate beings: that is how we can help others out of their pain and suffering. Having suffered a good deal of pain while making my transition from Chicago/New York, and the world of corporate human resources, to life as a consultant in Tucson, Arizona, the lessons of Buddhism resonated within me.

Kabbalah

My study of Jewish mysticism had begun long before I undertook my doctoral studies. The Kabbalah gave me a greater understanding of how all religions really are connected at the spiritual level.

What was the most poignant aspect of these studies for me, and how did that contribute to my understanding of conflict resolution? Similar to Buddhist philosophy, the Kabbalah views life as a journey. When there is evil or wrongdoing, it is not evil by itself; it is the absence of good. I translated that into the belief that people did not have to regard each other as evil; what we needed was to understand one another's perspectives. (Do not misunderstand: I am not naïve—I know there are evil people in the world.)

Therefore, the study of Kabbalah reminded me that in my design of a conflict resolution model, I needed to keep in mind that, underneath it all, we are all human. For me that translated to mean that when we are not intimidated by anyone or any situation, conflict resolution and personal transformation is possible for everyone.

After I completed my PhD, I used The Working Circle in both my work and volunteer activities. Over the years, I made modifications—not to the design, but to some of the language. The Circle has never failed me.

Subsequent to my formal studies, I digested and incorporated the concepts of emotional intelligence, especially the work of Daniel Goleman. Participants in my seminars loved hearing that emotional intelligence (i.e., the ability to resonate with people) was possible for all of us, no matter what intellectual capacity we are born with.

Acknowledgments

Gratitude fills me as I write these pages.

Thanks first to Claire Gerus, my agent, friend, and supporter, who stood by me even when I had given up. She resurrected my hope so I could follow my dream.

To Dan Ambrosio, my editor at Wiley: my gratitude extends to you as I continue to learn the meaning of collaboration. Thanks also to Ashley Allison, editorial assistant; Peter Knox, marketing; and Lauren Freestone, production editor.

My corporate experiences have been priceless. I learned at such a pace as to make me dizzy. From American Express to Chase Bank to KPMG Peat Marwick and, finally, Alexander & Alexander, they were all fantastic experiences, and I wouldn't trade them for anything. I worked for geniuses as well as kooks; all were teachers.

My thanks extend to all of my many clients across the United States and Mexico. They have been teachers and friends, as well as my working laboratory.

Closest to my heart are my friends, who have loved and supported me throughout: you know who you are. My parents, though gone for years, I know, are watching and sharing my pride at the chance I now have to spread good work to a wider audience. Special thanks to Martie Maierhauser, who helped me with editing the book. And, finally, to JLC, the person who has tamed my heart, led my fan club, and nurtured me beyond belief.

May we all find peace in our hearts and in the world in which we live.

Index